W9-CBY-527

START YOUR TRIP WITH A FULL TANK

Other Books by Ron Hutchcraft

Five Needs Your Child Must Have Met at Home
Letters from the College Front: Girls' Edition
Letters from the College Front: Guys' Edition
Peaceful Living in a Stressful World
Wake-Up Calls

START YOUR TRIP WITH A FULL TANK

AND OTHER SPIRITUAL JUMP STARTS

RON HUTCHCRAFT

Baker Books

A Division of Baker Book House Co
Grand Rapids, Michigan 49516

© 1996 by Ron Hutchcraft

Published by Baker Books
a division of Baker Book House Company
P.O. Box 6287, Grand Rapids, MI 49516-6287

Printed in the United States of America

All rights reserved. No part of this publication may be reproduced, stored in a retrieval system, or transmitted in any form or by any means—for example, electronic, photocopy, recording—without the prior written permission of the publisher. The only exception is brief quotations in printed reviews.

Library of Congress Cataloging-in-Publication Data

Hutchcraft, Ronald.
    Start your trip with a full tank : and other spiritual jump starts / Ron Hutchcraft.
    p. cm.
    ISBN 0-8010-5298-X (paper)
    1. Christian life. 2. Spiritual life—Christianity. 3. Love—Religious aspects—Christianity. 4. Success—Religious aspects—Christianity. 5. Interpersonal relations—Religious aspects—Christianity. I. Title.
BV4501.2.H874 1996
248.4—dc20   95-37014

Unless otherwise noted, Scripture quotations are from the HOLY BIBLE, NEW INTERNATIONAL VERSION ®. NIV ®. Copyright © 1973, 1978, 1984 by International Bible Society. Used by permission of Zondervan Publishing House. All rights reserved.

Quotes of Hudson Taylor on pages 190–91 taken from Hudson Taylor, *To China with Love: The Only Autobiographical Writing of J. Hudson Taylor* (Minneapolis: Bethany Fellowship, [1972]), 19–20.

To those precious friends, some known and some unknown, who "pray for you every day, Ron." You have given me a priceless gift and quietly made the difference in a thousand battles.

To one who prays for me daily: my dear mother, Jeanne, who was my cheerleader in so many growing up moments and who was my exclusive audience for the first things I ever wrote.

In loving memory of my wonderful father, John Hutchcraft, who prayed faithfully for me, who lovingly modeled Christian manhood for me, and who loyally believed in me.

Contents

Blow the Lid off Your Life!   11

The Power You Need:
Surprising Secrets of Personal Power

Why It's Taking So Long to Put It Together   16
A Price within Your Reach   18
Getting Your Mouth Open   20
Starting Your Trip with a Full Tank   22
Walking without Support   24
Only a Reflection   26
Good-Bye, Sick Stuff 28
Telling Isn't Trusting   30
"Stat" Living   32
Seeing Where the Wind Will Take You   34
Knowing When It's Time to Run   36
The Child Test   38
Right Answers under Pressure   40
The Desire to Disappear   42
The Problem's at the Source   44
Working without Leaving Home   46
Reaching through the Flames   48
The Silence of the Good Guys   50
Impressing God 52
No Third Choice   54

The Relationship You're Restless For:
Unleashing Your Relationship with God

"Congratulations! You've Been Chosen!"   58

Pursuing Your Master   60
"New" Is More Than a Smell   62
Stuck in a Holding Pattern   64
Energizer Christians   66
Your Sometimes-Shrieking, Sometimes-Laughing Mirror   68
Getting Out of the Way   70
A Place to Say "Yes!"   72
An Appropriate "Wow!"   74
The Face of Intimacy   76
Your Own Personal Umpire   78
Nothing without the Trigger   80
Disappointment Mountain   82
Looking Good, Going Nowhere   84
How to Beat the Distraction Action   86
The Galaxies and the Groceries   88
Always in Touch with the Tower   90
Casual Is Out   92
Something Old in Your New Beginning   94

The Hard Times That Hurt You: Winning When You're Hurting

Beautiful Scars   98
A Tower They Can't Blow Up   100
The Eeyore Complex   102
Music When You Least Expect It   104
The Mission Impossible Prayer   106
The Senioritis Vaccine   108
Reservation Tested   110
Clouds Blocking the Fireworks   112
The Hands Tell It All   114
Making Hell's List   116
Never Playing Defense   118
Pieces and Masterpieces   120
The Miracle Rush   122
Slow Down for Construction   124
When You Force It, You Break It   126

Accident or Assignment?   128
Father to the Finish   130
What to Do with Life's Dirty Words   132
Loyal in the Losing Seasons   134

The People You Love:
Deepening Your Relationship with Your Family

The Power of a Fist   138
Marriage Miracles   140
A Guidance System for the Missiles at Home   142
How to See through Your Blind Spot   144
Trampling on a Masterpiece   146
Getting In on Someone Else's Badge   148
The Irreplaceables   150
Control Freaks   152
The Container Hang-Up   154
The Rebuilder's Dream   156
The Only Safe Sex   158
Build Your Levee High   160
Light Vision   162
No Pilot, No Progress   164
Young People Leading the Charge   166
Noticeably Married   168
Tampering with the Pole That Holds It Up   170
My Father Is Missing   172

The "Tripper-Uppers" That Hinder You:
Conquering Your Dark Side

Facing What Could Hit You   176
The "I Can Handle It" Trap   178
Shower Power   180
The Shortcut Takes Too Long   182
Overlooking the Instructions   184
Uncovering the Mines   186
The Longer It Waits, the Harder It Gets   188

The Unstuffing Adventure   190
Hollow on the Inside   192
The Good Way to Get Bad News   194
When Shopping Costs Too Much   196
The First Channel Is the Worst Channel   198
Spun to the Edge   200
Find the Hole and Plug It   202
Plastic Wars   204
The Target on Your Back   206
Never without Your Weapon   208
Erasing Tattoos   210
Dying from Doing Nothing   212

The Mission You Were Made For: Living As a "Make a Difference" Person

Sleeping through the Feast   216
Nervous about Eternity   218
Soaking the Soaked   220
No Contact, No Transfer   222
Getting Through   224
When Lifeguards Forget the Beach   226
The Power Preposition   228
Going In with Backup   230
A Basketful of Earth   232
The Price Is Right   234
Leaving without a Fill-Up   236
None of Your Business   238
Undeniable Evidence   240
"Where's the Bullets?"   242
Words from Higher Up   244
Dead-End Applause   246
Darker Nights, Brighter Lights   248
Not Enough Days   250

Blow the Lid off Your Life!

Nuclear missiles. Those have been scary words ever since I was a kid. I knew America had some—and that other folks did too. Their missiles were pointed in our direction.

One day I was virtually right on top of a nuclear missile. I had been asked to speak at a northern frontier air force base that was home to 150 missiles with nuclear warheads. An officer took me on a "missile tour."

I knew those ICBMs were not sitting out there, towering over us like Cape Canaveral rockets on their launch pads. They are kept in underground silos, grimly primed for a moment everyone hopes will never come. The officer explained to me that if one of those missiles was launched, it would travel 6,000 miles to its programmed target!

It was interesting to learn that many of these missile silos were not on the base, but on private farms. We drove by one. No sign of any missile—just a concrete mound rising slightly above the ground. "That cover is solid concrete," the officer informed me. "It weighs many tons."

Well, my civilian imagination shifted into overdrive. A farm with a nuclear missile right under the cows and the corn. I thought, "It must make it easier for Farmer Jones to find a stray cow at night. She probably glows in the dark!"

Closer to reality, I thought, "Isn't that concrete lid going to cause a little problem when the missile is launched?" I imagined this great ball of fire and smoke, and then the missile going nowhere. Being a dumb civilian, I asked. Being a patient officer, he answered.

He explained that the silo cover was wired with explosives (I knew that, of course). Before the missile is launched, they detonate those explosives and blow that lid about forty yards laterally. My imagination couldn't help it—I could just picture some wide-eyed cow bellowing a loud, pitiful "mooooo-ooooo!" as it blew by.

Actually, I was fascinated with what I had seen and heard. That missile was built for a mission and loaded with power to accomplish it. But it could not achieve the orbit it was designed for until the lid was blown off. Neither can you.

Most of us are underliving—well below the powerful orbit our Creator designed us for. In fact, our hearts seem to whisper to us, "This isn't all there is. There's so much more!" We're tired of mediocrity . . . of sameness . . . of loneliness. In the world's best-selling Book, the Bible, our Creator pinpoints the reason for our restlessness—"He has also set eternity in the hearts of men" (Eccles. 3:11).

We're destined for something more than earth stuff, earth power, earth love. And Jesus Christ stands ready to give us the eternity we were created for. In His own words, "I have come that they may have life, and have it to the full" (John 10:10).

But like that missile, we have a lid holding us back from all that our hearts are hungry for. As you begin to walk through the pages of this book, I want to extend an invitation to you to *blow the lid off your life!*

Yes, there is more power than you have experienced. There is more love and intimacy, more significance. The secrets of the love and power we're hungry for await us in the timeless pages of God's Book, the Bible. For thousands of years, people have been "launched" into an exciting, empowering orbit by seeing their lives through their Creator's eyes.

"I've read the Bible," someone might say. "It's helpful, but I wouldn't say it's been that revolutionary." Many people have read the Bible, but they haven't let the Bible read them. Too often God's words make it to our heads, but not to our hearts . . . into our beliefs, but not into our lives.

It's like sugar. If you eat something like a candy bar, the sugar can have one of two results. If you eat it and then just lie on the couch, it will turn to fat. If you eat it and start exercising, it will turn to energy. The reason God's Word does not launch us to a higher orbit is that we tend just to store it rather than to put it to work. But when we immediately incorporate the Word of God into our everyday life, we are energized and changed by it. Repeat that process day after day for a period of time, and the lid will come off!

I extend to you this invitation to explore the deep corners of your life with the light of God's Word—yes, to let the Bible read you. Each day we will visit a practical life-issue and look at the difference Jesus could make in it. I have done my best to illuminate each day's "word from the Word of God" with a real-life example, and to suggest how you might put it to work today. I live every day believing that "this is my Father's world" and that we can see Him in thousands of everyday experiences.

Together, we will focus on six life arenas:

- The Power You Need: Surprising Secrets of Personal Power
- The Relationship You're Restless For: Unleashing Your Relationship with God
- The Hard Times That Hurt You: Winning When You're Hurting
- The People You Love: Deepening Your Relationship with Your Family
- The "Tripper-Uppers" That Hinder You: Conquering Your Dark Side
- The Mission You Were Made For: Living As a "Make a Difference" Person

Our mission in all of this—my observations and your applications—will be to connect God's words to the things that matter to you. The Bible does its powerful work only when it's connected to something in your life.

One day you will reach the last page of this book—and the first page of your book. It is my prayer that our daily visits will propel you into a lifetime of spiritual discovery, using the powerful combination of a God-statement from the Bible, an example from everyday life, and a personal application. Then you won't need my book. You'll be writing your own, perhaps in your own Jesus journal.

You cannot imagine the revolutionary impact of this daily time with Jesus through the words He wrote you. You will be steadily drawn more and more into the heart of your Creator. You will experience the power of letting God permeate and re-create the things that matter most to you. And you will begin to taste the exciting orbit you were designed for.

Your heart has been spiritually restless for greater things. Your loving Lord has been anxious to give them to you. As you open yourself up to His daily touch on your daily life, you will, as they say in the launch business, "have ignition."

The lid to your life is coming off!

THE POWER YOU NEED

**Surprising Secrets
of Personal Power**

When a little boy wants to play with his daddy, he can be pretty persistent. Billy sure was while his dad was trying to read the newspaper. Every couple of minutes, it seemed, Billy would ask, "Daddy, can we please go play hide-and-seek?"—which is the last thing his dad felt like doing. Finally, his dad thought, "How am I going to occupy him? I'm never going to get through this paper." Then he noticed a full-page ad in the paper that had a map of the world on the other side. "Aha! I know what I'll do." He tore it up into pieces and said, "Here, Billy. Why don't you put together this puzzle of the world, and when you have that together, come back and show me, and then I'll play with you." He settled back to finish his newspaper, and about three minutes later Billy came running back, and said, "Daddy, I got it all together." His dad looked, and it was all done. He said, "Billy, how did you put it together so fast?"

Well, Billy's secret might help you to put *your* puzzle together. Let's take a God-moment about . . .

Why It's Taking So Long to Put It Together

Our word from the Word of God comes from this stirring passage in 2 Chronicles 7:14. "If my people, who are called by my name, will humble themselves and pray and seek my face and turn from their wicked ways, then will I hear from heaven and will forgive their sin and will heal their land." This is a fascinating verse because it's an "If you, then I" statement. God says, "If you will meet these conditions, then I will do this." God says, "I am standing by, waiting to do some things in your life that I know you need done." He says, "I want to answer some prayer that maybe you have been waiting for months or years to be answered." So He says, "I will hear from heaven. I will forgive your sin. I want to give you that new beginning you have been looking for." He says, "I will heal your land. I want to fix the things or the people that are torn in your life." We say, "Well, God, please do." He says, "Well, if you, then I."

God gives four things He wants us to do. Humble ourselves, pray, seek His face, and turn from our wicked ways. Do you know what God seems to be saying? "Let Me work in you, then I can do those things for you. Before I can solve your puzzles, I have to solve *you*." When Billy came back with his puzzle, the map of the world his dad had torn up, his dad asked, "How did you put it together so quickly?" Billy said, "Daddy, there was a picture of a man on the other side, and when you put the man together right, the world goes together just fine." Maybe that is what God needs to do in your life to fix some of the problems you have been praying about. Humble yourself, which means you surrender the self-management of your life and surrender to a new dependency on Him. Stop pushing and nagging and scheming. Make prayer your major method of getting things done. Seek His face. Make sure your time with Him once again becomes the number-one priority of your schedule. Then turn from your wicked ways. He is saying, "Attack that sin, that compromise you've been tolerating, that attitude, that selfishness, that dark part of you. If you would let that be touched by Jesus, maybe that would start the healing."

Would you pray this? "Lord, what do You want to change, not in my situation, but in me?" The secret of your puzzle coming together may be just what that little boy discovered. Once the Man goes together, the world will go together just fine.

Have you ever noticed what happens when airlines lower their fares? First one airline declares a price war, and by the end of the day, everybody is having a sale. It's great! People who were not going to fly anywhere are suddenly booking tickets. Hank, who never flies, is now flying to see his cousin because he can't pass up the deal. Dave and his wife are traveling to California to see their granddaughter, whom they thought they wouldn't see for a long time. People gobble up these lowered fares in a couple of days, and the phones practically melt down at the airlines. Why? Because the discounts bring something within reach that we could otherwise never afford, and we act on it. Let's take a God-moment about . . .

A Price within Your Reach

Our word from the Word of God comes from Ephesians 2, beginning with verses 4 and 5. "Because of his great love for us, God, who is rich in mercy, made us alive with Christ even when we were dead in transgressions—it is by grace you have been saved." Verse 8 continues, "It is by grace you have been saved, through faith—and this not from yourselves, it is the gift of God—not by works, so that no one can boast."

What is God saying here? That we have been saved by *grace,* which can be defined as undeserved love. God's amazing, undeserved love, how sweet the sound! This passage is talking about our need to have our sins forgiven so we can have a relationship with God and go to heaven instead of hell.

This is good news and bad news. First, the bad news. There is no way we can afford forgiveness and eternal life. This passage says we are dead spiritually. And there is nothing a dead person can do to affect his or her situation. Discount fares may bring airline prices within reach, but in the case of our spiritual salvation, we can never pay the price. Our only hope is if

God does something to bring heaven within our reach, because our reach for God just doesn't come close.

Discount fares may bring airline prices within reach, but in the case of our spiritual salvation, we can never pay the price.

All of this might be a shock to you if you are a religious person. Maybe you've been a believer, you've done a lot of good, you've been through everything your religion asks of you, you have the approval of religious people, and you've paid a lot for a fare to heaven. Well, it won't get you there. "Not by works," Scripture says. Admitting that we cannot pay our own way to heaven is one of our biggest obstacles to overcome. But it can and must be done.

The first step is to say, "God, I'm lost. I'm bankrupt. I can't contribute anything to my salvation." Now you are ready to consider what Jesus did to bring salvation within your reach. *He paid the fare.* On the cross, He paid for your sins and was cut off from God so you don't have to be. Salvation's price could not be lowered so you could get it through your goodness. The full price had to be paid, and it was paid by the One we had sinned against. It is the gift of God, Ephesians says. That means saying, "I pin all my hopes on You, Jesus." If you have never done that, don't risk another day without God.

Jesus holds out the gift He bought with His life. He has brought it within your reach—a relationship with God you never could have paid for. Now it is time for you to reach out and take it. When something you cannot afford is brought within your reach, it is time for action, especially if that something is heaven.

Babies do not always know what is good for them, especially when it comes to food. That's why, rather than pry open a stubborn baby's mouth (which is not very effective and not very nice), we play airplane. We put the food on a spoon, pilot it slowly around, make the baby smile, then quickly land in the open mouth. Hopefully. Sometimes that hangar door suddenly closes, leaving the airplane's cargo all over the baby's face. What a crazy baby! I have what the baby needs, but he won't open his mouth. Let's take a God-moment about . . .

Getting Your Mouth Open

Our word from the Word of God comes from Psalm 81:10–16. Here's what God says. "I am the LORD your God, who brought you up out of Egypt. Open wide your mouth and I will fill it. But my people would not listen to me; Israel would not submit to me. So I gave them over to their stubborn hearts to follow their own devices. If my people would but listen to me, if Israel would follow my ways, how quickly would I subdue their enemies and turn my hand against their foes! . . . You would be fed with the finest of wheat; with honey from the rock I would satisfy you." Years ago God was saying to His people—and today He is saying to us—that His people are underliving. There is so much more He wants to give us and do for us. There is a voice inside of many of us that is saying, "There has got to be something more in this relationship with Christ and in this Christian living."

This is not news to make us materially prosperous, but to know that God has more power, more peace, more love, and more significance to open up our lives so we can really make a difference. The problem is, He can't get our mouths open, just like a baby being fed. God wants us to want His best for our lives. That's opening our mouths. He wants us to expect the supernatural and to act as if the supernatural is coming. In

Jesus' hometown, Nazareth, "he did not do many miracles . . . because of their lack of faith" (Matt. 13:58). He did miracles everywhere but there, and the people who knew the most about Him saw the least supernaturally because they weren't expecting anything. They didn't open their mouths. Faith is acting as if God will keep His promise and do something God-sized. God says, "I tried to, and they would not listen. They would not follow My ways."

Is there a part of your life where you have been doing your own thing and going your own way? Maybe at home, at work, at church, in your love life, or with your finances. Perhaps in your relationships you're missing God's best because you're going your own way. He says, "I've let them follow their own devices." In that part of your life, you're on your own, settling for crumbs when He wants to serve you a banquet.

Instead, why don't you start living as if you want God's best, trusting Him for His best? He is holding in His hands the supernatural food you need right now. Just open your mouth, and let Him fill it.

One of the real highlights for our family is our family trips. A lot of memories are made on those vacations, and they're great . . . once we get going. The problem is that getting ready is such a production. First we have to decide where to go. That's a huge task, because with five different people with five different interests, where are we going to go?! When we get that settled, we have to pack. Of course, you have to pack for the weather you have here, and you have to pack for the weather on the other end, which might be different. Then we have to figure out what's going to happen with the newspaper, the bird, and the dog while we're gone. Of course, car problems we've postponed fixing have to all be fixed. We have to get the snacks together. Yes, we need money, so we get to the bank. Oh, and most important, we fill the gas tank. Our rule is, once we get going on a trip, we want enough gas to make sure we can keep going. Let's take a God-moment about . . .

Starting Your Trip with a Full Tank

Our word from the Word of God comes from Psalm 90:14, where David prays this simple prayer. "Satisfy us in the morning with your unfailing love." Well, David is a realist. He knows the reality of real life: It's lived out in days. We don't have a life, we have days. So he says, "Lord, every morning, at the beginning of each of these twenty-four-hour things called days, I need You to satisfy me with Your unfailing love." And as the morning goes, so goes the day. It's like the old saying, "It's the set of the sail, not the force of the gale, that determines the way you go." Our sail gets set in those first moments of the day. This verse is saying that we need to fill our tanks with God's unfailing love before we start our trip through the day—and before we see anybody else. David echoes this in Psalm 143:8. "Let the morning bring me word of your unfailing love." In Psalm

59:16 he says, "In the morning I will sing of your love." Get the idea? In the morning, I have to fill up with His love.

See, each day is a long trip, with stress, surprises, and people pulling at us; and it's tempting to just take off on the trip without that time with Jesus, or cutting that time short. We can't afford that. We have to protect that time with Him; and I think it's important to not just be around Him, not just read verses about Him, but make sure we touch His unfailing love and hear

---

We need to fill our tank with God's unfailing love before we start our trip through the day.

Him say to us, "I love you. I love you today. I love you no matter what." That's our emotional fill-up for our tank. I also think we need to get on our knees for that. Literally, physically, get on our knees, get on our face as many people did in the Bible, and allow ourselves to not just be with a book but really be with Jesus. He's going to say, "I love you unfailingly."

Now, you may not know where you stand with everybody else in your world today, but you can be secure in His love. There's one relationship in which you can totally unmask and totally be you. There is no fear of rejection, because His love is unfailing. Visit the cross every morning, and remember how loved you are. Park your doubts right there. You don't know what the day is going to hold, but you do know that Someone loves you totally and that He has okayed everything that is going to come into your day. This is the day that not my boss, the weather, or my teachers have made; but this is the day my Lord has made.

You have too many demands in your daily trip to miss filling up with God's love for you. Be with Him intimately enough every morning to know His love. That's your emotional fuel. "Jesus loves me, this I know." The alternative is running out of emotional gas before your trip is over, so start with a full tank.

Our family got to go to a premiere together. Actually, it was in a living room, and it was the premiere of the Hutchcraft family movies transferred to videotape. We watched one movie of our older son, Doug, learning to walk. Here he was as a little guy, toddling around, with his big sister, Lisa, trying to help him. He would grab on to the little coffee table in the middle of the floor, then he'd reach for the couch, and next he'd hold his sister's hand. Finally, he was walking—but only if he could hang on to some support. It was cute to see him walk like that then. It would not be cute today, though, if he couldn't walk unless he could hold on to something. I'm really proud of him because he gets around pretty well now. How did he learn to really walk? Well, here's Dad over there, encouraging him. You can't hear it, but you can kind of see, "Come on, Doug. Come on. Come to Daddy." Doug's looking at his dad, and finally he lets go of all his props and in this victorious moment, walks across the floor. It was worth the film just to have that shot! Walking by ourselves is an important milestone in growing up. Let's take a God-moment about . . .

Walking without Support

Our word from the Word of God comes from Matthew 14, beginning at verse 25. The disciples are being thrown around by a terrible storm on the Sea of Galilee. "During the fourth watch of the night Jesus went out to them, walking on the lake. When the disciples saw him walking on the lake, they were terrified. 'It's a ghost,' they said, and cried out in fear. But Jesus immediately said to them: 'Take courage! It is I. Don't be afraid.' 'Lord, if it's you,' Peter replied, 'tell me to come to you on the water.' 'Come,' he said. Then Peter got down out of the boat, walked on the water and came toward Jesus. But when he saw the wind, he was afraid and, beginning to sink, cried out, 'Lord, save me!' Immediately Jesus reached out his hand and caught him." Peter walks where there is no apparent means of support, like Doug did as a baby. It looks scary, but letting go is a giant step forward in the things we can do with our lives. Now, most of us insist on staying in the boat. Eleven disciples stayed in the boat, while only one had the faith to get out. But we can only go so far with Jesus without taking risks. The really powerful stuff starts to happen when we step out.

But we can only go so far with Jesus without taking risks. The really powerful stuff starts to happen when we step out.

Right now, maybe the Lord is asking you to take a miracle walk. There's no visible means of support. He's calling you to step away from the people, the places, or maybe the security you've always held on to. If so, you need to remember four essentials when going into a miracle walk. Number one, check with Jesus. Peter said, "Lord, if it's you." Make sure it's the Lord who is asking you to step out of the boat. Confirm that in prayer, through His Word, and through counsel. It doesn't matter how hard the wind blows. It doesn't matter if there is no visible means of support. It doesn't matter if no one has ever done it before, if Jesus is asking you to do it. Second, abandon safety. You have to get out of the boat and out of the safe comfy spot you've been in. Third, walk on water. Start stepping out into the new ground, or water, where you've never stepped before. Fourth, focus on Jesus, not on the situation, the wind, the storm, or the things you fear. Do what Peter failed to do when he was halfway to Jesus. Keep dwelling on the One who called you out of the boat in the first place instead of on what is outside the boat.

When Doug finally took that risk and walked where there was no support, he achieved a major milestone in his growth. Now, if Jesus is asking you to do that, you're on the edge of a quantum leap in your life. You're about to abandon the natural and taste the supernatural.

Some of God's most impressive artwork is hidden underwater or underground. He cannot make boring stuff, even if it is in a place where few people will ever see it. Scuba divers know all about God's extravagant beauty, and I was reminded of it when our family toured some caverns. What rare beauty we saw in soaring stalagmites, underground canyons, and unique rock formations. But the highlight was a little pond called Mirror Lake. It's only about six inches deep, but it looks much deeper. Looking into this glasslike pond, you see a vast assortment of big and small rock formations that appear to be under the water. It's hard to believe at first, but actually they are on the ceiling of the cave above the lake. The beauty in that lake is really just a reflection of the beauty above the lake. Let's take a God-moment about being . . .

Only a Reflection

Our word from the Word of God comes from 2 Corinthians 3:18. It is about reflected beauty. "And we, who with unveiled faces all reflect the Lord's glory, are being transformed into his likeness with ever-increasing glory, which comes from the Lord, who is the Spirit." This refers to Exodus 34, where Moses had come down from the mountain after being in the personal presence of the Lord and "his face was radiant because he had spoken with the LORD" (v. 29). The glow was on Moses. It wasn't from Moses, but it was sure on him. He spent time with the Lord, and as a result, he began to reflect the Lord's glory and didn't even realize it.

Now, Mirror Lake, in that dark cavern, has little beauty of its own. It's really an underground puddle. But it reflects the beauty of what is above it, and that makes it come to life. The same thing can happen to us, if we have a personal relationship with Jesus Christ and are spending time with Him. If we allow Him to transform us and make us more like Him, it is possible for us ordinary human beings to have an extraordinary impact on someone's life simply because we display Jesus to them.

Here are some important reminders if you want to be one of God's mirrors. First, be with Jesus daily, with the purpose of that time together being to let Him change you. Say, "Lord, how can You make me a little more like You today?" Second, be confident because of whom you represent. You don't have

---

He spent time with the Lord, and as a result, he began to reflect the Lord's glory and didn't even realize it.

---

to focus on your appearance, your ability, your limitations, or the impression you're making. If you focus on the incredible Savior you are trying to display, you will become a more confident person. Third, be committed to leaving people focused on Jesus rather than on yourself. Do you want people to think about the puddle, or the beauty the puddle reflects? Finally, be tough on any self-glorifying thoughts. If you find yourself saying, "Hey, aren't I something?" after something good happens, then you are on the way down. You need to say, "Lord, aren't You something!"

The words of an old hymn say, "May His beauty rest upon me as I seek the lost to win, and may they forget the channel, seeing only Him." So, Mirror Lake Person, don't be too impressed with yourself. Don't promote yourself. And don't be too impressed with other people, or you will be too intimidated to show them Jesus. Be impressed with the glory of Jesus above you—and that He wants to show it to everyone else through you.

When I get sick, it is a rare event in our family. I feel blessed with a pretty healthy life. But once, when I was hit with the flu, I was too weak to talk or even turn over. Finally, about twenty-four hours later, I started to improve. When I began to feel better, I desperately wanted a shower, and that was my first physical triumph after the battle with the flu. I happily piled in a corner the symbol of that long, dark day I'd had—those blue flannel pajamas I had worn the whole time. They had been sweated out several times, and they didn't smell very nice. They probably should have been burned. Now, I was showered, with fresh clean clothes on. I would not have put those rotten, old pajamas back on for anything. Let's take a God-moment about saying . . .

Good-Bye, Sick Stuff

Our word from the Word of God comes from John 11, beginning at verse 38. Here Jesus faces one of the great challenges of His ministry. His good friend Lazarus has died, and weeping friends and family have gathered around the tomb. The Bible says: "Jesus, once more deeply moved, came to the tomb. It was a cave with a stone laid across the entrance. 'Take away the stone,' he said." They did, although Martha objected, "By this time there is a bad odor, for he has been there four days." Verse 43 says, "Jesus called in a loud voice, 'Lazarus, come out!' The dead man came out, his hands and feet wrapped with strips of linen, and a cloth around his face. Jesus said to them, 'Take off the grave clothes and let him go.'"

Can you imagine Lazarus returning later to get back into his old grave clothes? I am sure he would not return to the stuff that was wrapped around him while he was dead, just as I would not have put my flu pajamas back on. Yet, in a way, many of us do that very thing. We are all like Lazarus, because we have all been raised from the living death of trying to make it without Christ. According to 2 Corinthians 5:17, we are new creatures in Christ. The old is gone, a new life has begun, and we leave our old grave clothes once and for all.

Could it be that you have drifted back to some of the old you? That habit you had beaten, are you flirting with it again? That compromising relationship you had finally put behind you, are you running around the edges of it again? That dark temper you had under Christ's control, is it now rearing its head again? Maybe it is that tendency to use people, hurt people, or walk over people. Maybe that side of you that takes matters into your own hands instead of trusting God to do it is reappearing. All of us have these empty, corrupt ways of living, but Christ comes and says, "Let him go. Take off the grave clothes." We can be free of them forever because of Jesus.

If you are drifting back to your grave clothes, stop and really remember what dead felt like. Return to the cross, where you were freed in the first place, and let Jesus say again, "Let him go!" When you are finally getting well, there is no reason in the world to go back to the sick stuff.

At my house, we joke that my nickname is Lo Tech, because my gifts are not technical or mechanical. I'm the first to admit that, so when something goes wrong with our car, I head for Dave's gas station. Dave has worked on our cars for years. He does a good job, and since I have been Joe Used Car most of my life, there is usually a fair amount of work to do. I come chugging in and tell Dave the symptoms of what seems to be wrong with the car. I tell him about the noise, the starting problem, or the loss of power, and Dave tells me what he thinks it might be, what he thinks it might cost, and how long it might take to fix it. So what do I do? Do I say, "Thanks, Dave," and then chug out in my ailing car? No, I leave it there! Let's take a God-moment about how . . .

Telling Isn't Trusting

Our word from the Word of God comes from Luke 7, beginning at verse 2. "A centurion's servant, whom his master valued highly, was sick and about to die. The centurion heard of Jesus and sent some elders of the Jews to him, asking him to come and heal his servant. When they came to Jesus, they pleaded earnestly with him." At this point, they are telling Jesus about the problem, just like I tell Dave about my car's problem. Jesus goes with the elders, but the centurion sends a message back, "'Lord, don't trouble yourself, for I do not deserve to have you come under my roof. That is why I did not even consider myself worthy to come to you. But say the word, and my servant will be healed. For I myself am a man under authority, with soldiers under me. I tell this one, "Go," and he goes; and that one, "Come," and he comes. I say to my servant, "Do this," and he does it.' When Jesus heard this, he was amazed at him, and turning to the crowd following him, he said, 'I tell you, I have not found such great faith even in Israel.' Then the men who had been sent returned to the house and found the servant well."

Look at the words "such great faith." Jesus always talks to His disciples about their little faith. He says, "This unlikely man, a Gentile, has such great faith." Why? Well, he didn't just tell Jesus about the problem, he trusted Him with it. That's why he got the miracle he needed.

It doesn't do any good if I just tell my mechanic about the problems my car has. I have to leave it in his hands and drive away in another car. I leave it there. I trust him. Maybe you are looking at a problem or a need that really could use the touch of God right now. You say, "Well, I've prayed about it a lot." You've prayed about it, but have you really left it with Him? You told Him, but have you trusted Him? Notice, the centurion says, "Just say the word, and it will be done." He recognizes the total authority of Jesus over the situation and acts as if it is totally in Jesus' hands. That is great faith.

Is that how you are when you pray about someone or something? "Lord, if You say come, it will come. If You say go, it will go. If You say do this, it will be done." Now, when Jesus has the problem, you don't have it anymore. When you tell Jesus about it, you walk in the throne room bent over with the load, and you walk out still bent over. No! When you really trust Jesus with it, you walk in bent over, but you walk out standing tall. You leave your load in Jesus' hands.

So relax in His total authority. Exercise the faith that brings down the supernatural—"such great faith." The old song says, "I must tell Jesus all of my troubles." Upgrade that to "I must trust Jesus." Drive it to Jesus, and then leave it with Him.

We better go to the emergency room" is one of my least favorite sentences. I'm glad our local hospital has an emergency room, but I do hate to go there. Not too long ago, our son had a mild stomach disorder, and the doctor decided it should be checked out. It happened over the weekend when he wasn't in, so we went—real late at night—to the emergency room. It was rush hour when we got there, so we had to take a number. We had already waited awhile for some medical attention, when finally a nurse and doctor noticed we were there. But suddenly every doctor and nurse in the emergency room dropped everything and vanished into another room. They had heard somebody yell, "Stat!" That is the word for a life-or-death emergency, so everybody went running. "Stat" means it is time to drop everything. Let's take a God-moment about . . .

"Stat" Living

Our word from the Word of God comes from Ephesians 5:15–16. "Be very careful, then, how you live—not as unwise but as wise, making the most of every opportunity, because the days are evil." I looked up these verses in the Greek, and the word that says, "Be very careful how you live," literally means "walking around." Be very careful how you walk around. Make sure you look very carefully at your everyday activities and all the things that you're doing. Check everything out.

Then Paul says to live smart. Don't be unwise. Live smart, and live wisely. What does it mean to live in a way that God calls smart? By making the most of every opportunity, and here the Greek means "buying up the time." You can tell how wise people are by how they use their time.

How do you use yours? If you live by the motto "I have no time to waste," then you are living wisely. Why? "Because the days are evil." That word *evil* literally means "sick." The world around us is a sick and dying place. Your school is an emergency room. Where you work or in your neighborhood, people are terminal.

Do you know the song "People Need the Lord"? It's time we started putting names in that song. Bill needs the Lord. Kim needs the Lord. There's not much time left on God's clock, is

---

We need to be buying up our days like a shopper would grab the last item on sale.

---

there? Besides, God only gives us on average seventy years to live a life that will count for all eternity. I cannot waste a day. I cannot waste a conversation. I cannot waste an opportunity or a relationship. We need to be buying up our days like a shopper would grab the last item on sale.

Once a lady said to me, "Ron, I've been living for the Lord, but for thirty years I've been wasting time on soap operas, and it's going to be hard to give them up." Then she said, "I can't waste that kind of time anymore." It's time to evaluate. What are the time wasters in your life? This is war! We cannot mess around with trivial pursuits when bullets are flying.

God is looking at your world and yelling, "Stat!" It calls for a life-and-death immediate response. It is time to live, not casually, but urgently.

Happiness is a sailboat. Well, I have some friends who believe that. They work in high-stress environments all week long, and they let it all go on their sailboats on their day off. I know a few who have big sailboats, but most of them have the little Sunfish type. It isn't much, but it's all they need to get out on that lake. They'll go alone, or if they have room, they'll get a couple of friends, which is how I got to go a few times. Now, if you just have a boat and a mast, you're going to sit there until you're older. The action really begins when you put up the sail. That's when it gets exciting because you wait to see where the wind will take you. Let's take a God-moment about . . .

Seeing Where the Wind Will Take You

Our word from the Word of God comes from Psalm 37:5. "Commit your way to the LORD; trust in him and he will do this." Pretty simple instructions, aren't they? We could breeze right by them, taking them as a nice little motto. But this really says that we need to take the way we're going today and turn it over to the Lord. Too many of us let our relationship with Him deteriorate into something general, boring, theological, or theoretical. See, the lifestyle God suggests here is alive. It's practical. It's as practical as all the things we have to do today. This makes our to-do list God's to-do list, our appointments His appointments, our purchases His purchases, as we consciously commit them to Him before we get to them.

So at the beginning of the day, pray through your day. In other words, just before you ever go out and start all the things that make up your day, go into it mentally and visit each part of it and each person you know you're going to be involved with. Visit it consciously with Jesus, go there with Jesus, and make Him Lord over each of the places you expect to go, of each of the things you expect to do, of each of the people you expect to be around. Commit your way to the Lord.

But there's more to this daily adventure of following Jesus. Let Him surprise you. Along the way, as you commit your way to Him, you're saying, "Lord, since it's Your way, it's Your day. This is the day that the Lord has made, I'm going to rejoice

---

Don't lock up your day so tight that there's no room for God to insert a divine interruption or an unexpected opportunity to touch someone's life.

---

and be glad in it. You can make any changes You want. Maybe it won't go the way I planned it." Don't lock up your day so tight that there's no room for God to insert a divine interruption or an unexpected opportunity to touch someone's life. Maybe there even will be an unpleasant surprise that will set you up for a later blessing. It's good to have a way to give to the Lord. The idea is not that you just get up and drift all day with no course—that's a good way to end up on the rocks, and if you do, don't blame God for your lack of planning. Just give your way to the Lord to do with it as He knows best. Father really does know best.

In a sense, we're all supposed to be sailors, Holy Spirit sailors. Each morning, put up your sail and say, "Take me where You want to go today, Lord." Let the wind of God's Holy Spirit drive your day in the direction it's supposed to go.

Our son-in-law can sit still for only so long. Once while he was visiting us, he reached his sedentary limit, so he grabbed his basketball and went out to the hoop in our backyard. Now, it is a primitive basketball setup, with a home-made wooden backboard made of several boards affixed to a tree. He was working up a sweat out there, shooting and drib-bling, when suddenly he noticed a big bee buzzing around his head. He realized it had come from around the hoop and the backboard. Upon closer inspection, he saw a beehive there. Apparently those bees were not happy about that bas-ketball causing repeated hive quakes, and they were starting to respond. Now, Rick told me he knew what to do. He didn't try to ignore the bees and keep playing. He didn't try to kill the bees. He ran into the house as fast as he could. Let's take a God-moment about . . .

Knowing When It's Time to Run

Our word from the Word of God comes from 2 Timothy 2:22. "Flee the evil desires of youth, and pursue righteousness, faith, love and peace." Lots of people end up in sexual sins they thought they would never commit. Very few people of character plan to fall into sexual sin, whether it's going farther than God's and their standards would allow, premarital sex, or adultery.

I once began a radio program talking about statistics of how many young people have had premarital sex. Soon afterwards, a young radio listener wrote to me, pouring out her heart. She said, "Until a month ago, I never dreamed I would be one of those statistics." She went on about how she had made a series of choices that brought her into a situation where she was vul-nerable and where there was an opportunity to sin. She never wanted to, she never planned to, but she did, and now she was really hurting. It was a heartbreaking letter. This verse addresses how to avoid that: "Flee the evil desires of youth."

There are three things we can do with sexual temptation. First, we can flirt with it. This would be like our son-in-law, Rick, if he'd climbed on a ladder, inspecting that beehive and seeing how close he could get without getting stung. That would be dumb, and it is dumb when we try to do that with sexual temptation. The Bible calls sexual desire "fire in your lap." That's pretty explicit language to describe how we are only going to get burned if we flirt with fire.

The second thing we can do is fight sexual temptation. This would have Rick staying out there, still shooting his baskets, just trying to swat or kill every bee. Sexual desire will almost always ultimately win, unless we get away from it. It will over-power us if we allow ourselves to be in a situation where we can dwell on it, act on it, or be around it for very long.

The third thing we can do is what the Bible says to do. Flee from it. Be realistic. Do not underestimate sexual temptation or our ability to fall. Don't get anywhere close to it. We are never going to win morally unless we get as far from sexual temptation as possible. The girl in that letter spoke for millions who have had sex before marriage or outside their marriage vows. She said, "It just isn't worth it."

So get rid of any input that feeds your lust, whether a video-tape, music, magazines, humor, or television. Avoid settings where you are alone with someone of the opposite sex for any extended time. Change what you're doing at the first thought of anything wrong. Rick was smart. He knew you don't flirt with or even fight something that can really sting you. He ran. That's the way to win against temptation. Too many people have already been stung.

Paul is the Romeo of his high school class. There are taller and better looking guys than Paul, but he's been very successful with the ladies. He has a couple of advantages. First, he talks. Many guys just grunt, but Paul's able to talk and communicate with people, and the girls like that. He told me another secret. He said, "Ron, I really know how to handle babies and little kids." He hugs them, plays with them, and talks with them. He said, "The girls love it when you're nice to children." They're not the only ones. Let's take a God-moment about . . .

The Child Test

Our word from the Word of God comes from Mark 9. The disciples have just been arguing over who is going to be the greatest. Who will be the assistant Messiah? Who is going to have the top position? Jesus answers in an interesting way. He says, "'If anyone wants to be first, he must be the very last, and the servant of all.' He took a little child and had him stand among them. Taking him in his arms, he said to them, 'Whoever welcomes one of these little children in my name welcomes me; and whoever welcomes me does not welcome me but the one who sent me'" (vv. 35–37). Apparently it isn't just girls who want to see how we treat little children. This is a test of greatness in Jesus' eyes.

You want to be great? Be a servant. You want to be a servant? Show how you treat children. Why is that so important? Because to be a leader for Jesus, we don't promote ourselves, we promote other people. We make ourselves available for their needs. And nowhere does this show up more than in how we respond to a child. They have no money. They have no influence. They have no votes. So the issue is, How do you treat people who can't do a thing for you? For many adults, a child is a bother and a nonperson. "Get out of here, kid." A child is often in the way of our adult business, but they are supposed to be our most important adult business.

That day when the disciples knew that Jesus was having a summit conference with the leaders from Jerusalem, they said, "Oh, kids, please, don't bother Jesus. He's with the important people." Jesus said, "Wait a minute. They are the important people. Let them come to Me."

If we are going to be like Jesus, we have to learn to make children feel important. A child ought to be regarded as a VIP instead of a nuisance or a nonentity. So take time to learn children's names and to find out about their world. That world is as important to them as yours is to you. Ask them questions. Admire their primitive writing, art, or sculpture, and come down to their level, even physically. Take time to enter the world where they live. Children are brushed off so often by adults; you will be remembered if you take time for them.

Jesus said we practice servanthood on children, then we extend this Christlike humility to people in need, people who annoy us, interrupt us, and who can't do anything for us. If we can't pass the child test, we will never be servants. If we can't pass the servant test, we will never make a difference for our Lord. So stop for the children. Listen to the children. Respect the children. Jesus said He takes very personally the way you treat these little people who He thinks are big.

I never really liked TV game shows until my son got interested in one. It comes on after the evening news, which is what I watch on television. Maybe you have seen it—*Jeopardy*. What an appropriate title for a show that comes on right after the world news! Three contestants are given several categories, ranging from U.S. presidents to cat food. First a contestant picks a dollar value in a given category, and the host provides the answer. Then the three contestants vie to see who can be first to phrase the question that fits the answer. Some of them do very well and win lots of money—I saw one man who won fifty thousand dollars. But others fold. I said to my son, "Look at some of these people. They wind up in a hole with their money. How do they get on the show?" My compassionate son reminded me, "Dad, it's hard to come up with right answers when you have all that pressure on you." Let's take a God-moment about . . .

Right Answers under Pressure

We all know the feeling of the *Jeopardy* contestants. We've been in a conversation with our boss or our parents, we've dealt with one of our children on a key issue, we've tried to speak to a friend about the Lord, and the right answer is really important.

Nehemiah knew that feeling. Our word from the Word of God is in Nehemiah 2:1–5. Nehemiah, the king's cupbearer, was a Jewish exile in Persia. He had heard of the poor shape that his city, Jerusalem, was in, and he had a burden from the Lord to go and rebuild it. He knew he would need the king's help. He knew he would need time off. He didn't quite know how he would bring it up with the king. "I took the wine and gave it to the king. I had not been sad in his presence before; so the king asked me, 'Why does your face look so sad when you are not ill? This can be nothing but sadness of heart.' I was very much afraid, but I said to the king, 'May the king live forever! Why should my face not look sad when the city where my fathers are buried lies in ruins, and its gates have been destroyed by fire?' The king said to me, 'What is it you want?'" Drumroll. "Then I prayed to the God of heaven, and I answered the king." From this point on, the king becomes his ally in this great, historic cause. Here is a conversation that actually changed the course of history.

Our issues probably aren't that important, but we still need God's help. Here is how He displays His hand in important

---

Ask God for an open door, and then look for the openings.

---

conversations. First, we feel a divine nudge. Nehemiah had been praying about this situation for some time, so God said, "There is a need I want addressed through you, Nehemiah." God will put a burden on our hearts. Second, we are presented with a natural opportunity. When we wonder, "How in the world am I going to bring this up?" we need to ask God for a natural opportunity. The king asked Nehemiah the magic question, "What is it you want?" Ask God for an open door, and then look for the openings. Third, we receive an inspired answer from God. Nehemiah gave a tremendous answer to the king's question. It launched a whole chain of events. The key is what Nehemiah did, "I prayed to the God of heaven, and I answered the king."

Talk to the God of heaven before you talk to the person on earth. Connect yourself to the throne room. Then, even if you are scared, follow through with the opportunity God opens up. We must all play *Jeopardy* and come up with right answers under pressure, but we have a direct pipeline to the One who has all the right answers. Let Him come up with the answer.

In more than thirty years of youth ministry, I have done some strange things, many of which I would never do again. Some were associated with a camp activity known as the counselor hunt, when the kids are locked up for a few minutes and the counselors find a spot to hide. It seemed that they always would put a high price on my head, and if a team found me they got extra points. This gave me all the more incentive to not be found. I was *determined* to not let those campers find me. I would even scout out the perfect place during the day. One time, I ended up underneath a heavy, old enamel bathtub that another counselor flipped over on me. I was trapped under there for forty-five minutes with a mosquito that sounded like a B-52 bomber. I never could find him, and I couldn't turn on my flashlight because the kids would have found me. Another time I hid in a garbage can with all the garbage piled on top of me. Then there was the time I stashed myself in a shaft with a manhole cover on it, and the air got thinner and thinner. Crazy stuff. What, besides a touch of insanity, would motivate a grown man to do things like that? A strong desire to disappear. Let's take a God-moment about . . .

The Desire to Disappear

Our word from the Word of God comes from John 3:30. John the Baptist simply says, when speaking of Jesus, "He must become greater; I must become less." Understand that John is the center of attention at this point, probably receiving more attention than Jesus. He's front-page news. He's the best known preacher of his day. Many even say he is the Messiah. Yet, at the peak of his career, John says, "I don't want you to see me. I want to disappear. I want you to see Jesus." I am reminded of those words from Matthew 17:8 about the Mount of Transfiguration. "When they looked up, they saw no one except Jesus." Moses and Elijah had been there, back from heaven, but the disciples saw only Jesus. That ought to be the goal of everyone who ever does anything for Jesus Christ—to disappear and leave people thinking only about Jesus. We need to say, "He must become greater, I must become less." People will still see us because they know us and can touch, see, and hear us. They will trust us first. Our goal must always be to transfer that loyalty and attention to our Savior.

We need to say, "He must become greater, I must become less."

That is what happens when we allow a total Holy Spirit takeover before we minister. We begin to disappear. But when our flesh and our ego energize things, we want people to remember us, notice us, and think highly of us.

A lot of insecure people do things in Jesus' name, hoping their name will be promoted. Let it be your new prayer to disappear when you speak about Jesus to someone. Pray that you will be so Spirit-controlled and so in love with Jesus that they will see only Him. If you teach, sing, lead, preach, or counsel, don't tie people to you. Don't draw the attention to you. Tie them to the Lord Jesus Christ. He is the only One who deserves the spotlight. Get your ego out of the way, and you will find that as you disappear, the promise in 1 Peter 5:6 will come true: "Humble yourselves, therefore, under God's mighty hand, that he may lift you up in due time." When you have just done something for the Lord, the greatest compliment anyone could give you is "You disappeared today."

am okay with my computer until there is a problem. My computer once started going crazy—the power button was flashing, and it even started beeping. I thought it was going to blow. Actually, I did know that the computer acts this way when the battery power is running out. But I couldn't figure out why it was doing that then because I had plugged it in. I checked, and sure enough, the plug was in the power strip underneath the desk. The beeping was still going on, the warnings were still going off, and I was about to lose a lot of work. Now, my wife, Karen, knows more about this computer than I do, so I yelled, "Help!" She came in and quickly crawled under the desk, muttering, "If there's a problem, you have to start at the power source." The problem? The *power strip* wasn't turned on. Duh! Let's take a God-moment about how . . .

The Problem's at the Source

Our word from the Word of God comes from Mark 9. Jesus has just come down from the Mount of Transfiguration only to encounter a demon-filled young man and his father, who were desperately seeking Jesus' help. The disciples had tried to exercise their authority over this demon, but it wasn't working, so Jesus casts it out. Beginning in verse 28 Scripture says, "After Jesus had gone indoors, his disciples asked him privately, 'Why couldn't we drive it out?' He replied, 'This kind can come out only by prayer.'" In a sense, Jesus says what Karen told me about my computer, "If there's a problem, you have to start at the power source."

We are so much like the disciples. We try to do the right thing. We work at it, hit it with our best shot, but nothing happens. What is the problem? It's at the power source. We need to follow our cords back to the source by spending time on our knees in the throne room of God. Because for a Christian, a failure of power is almost always a failure to pray. Too often, prayer is an afterthought. We plan, we get on the phone, we talk to people with all the human resources, we make arrangements, we have committee meetings, and we work long hours. But Psalm 127 says, "Unless the LORD builds the house, its builders labor in vain. . . . In vain you rise early and stay up late."

Dr. Bob Cook, the late president of Youth for Christ and the King's College, said years ago, "Prayer is a method for getting things done." Prayer is not just something to *help* our methods. Hear Jesus saying, "Only by prayer." "If my people, who

---

We need to follow our cords back to the source by spending time on our knees in the throne room of God. Because for a Christian, a failure of power is almost always a failure to pray.

---

are called by my name, will humble themselves and pray . . ." (2 Chron. 7:14), that is when God hears from heaven and heals our land. God is not calling us to more effort. He is calling us to more prayer.

You and your mate need to be praying together. You and your church need to be praying together. You and your Christian coworkers, as well as your son or your daughter, need to pray together. God can do in a moment what people cannot do in fifty years.

So if the lights are blinking and the warning signals are sounding, you have a power problem. Get on your knees to find the answer. The prayer of faith turns on the power switch in the throne room of God.

Nowadays you don't have to physically go to work anymore, just like our friend Linda. The work comes to her. When you call her company's office, the company operator answers. You ask, "May I speak to Linda?" and she says, "Just a moment, please." You are on hold, and in a moment, you're talking to Linda. Who would suspect she's not there? She's working from her home. Since her baby was born, they transfer the calls right to her home, and nobody knows. Now, they have a name for this. It's called telecommuting. All you have to do is commute to your telephone to get to work. Everyone can contact you at your business number, and they never know you are not in the office. Telecommuting is making it possible for mothers to work at home, and it is also great for disabled people. There is so much people can accomplish right where they live. Let's take a God-moment about . . .

Working without Leaving Home

Our word from the Word of God comes from Exodus 17. The Jewish army is on a battlefield, fighting the savage Amalekites. Moses, who watches the scene from on top of a hill, is key to the victory. "As long as Moses held up his hands, the Israelites were winning, but whenever he lowered his hands, the Amalekites were winning" (v. 11). In verse 13, it says, "Joshua overcame the Amalekite army with the sword," so apparently Moses was able to keep his arms up enough. That was because two men went up there and *helped* him hold his arms up when they were drooping. After the battle, "Moses built an altar and called it The LORD is my Banner. He said, 'For hands were lifted up to the throne of the LORD.'" He was praying when his hands were lifted.

Now, Moses was too old to carry a sword into the battle. He wasn't really a soldier anyway, but that didn't mean he couldn't do something to affect the battle. He went up on that hill and raised his hands in prayer to the Lord. In fact, the Israelites won only when he did that. So we could call prayer God's powerful version of telecommuting. A precious eighty-five-year-old friend told me the other day, "Ron, I pray for you every day." That is the greatest gift she could give me. Going into God's throne room and bringing our fellow believers there in prayer is the greatest gift we can give them. Some people say, "All I can do is pray." What?! Go into the throne room and bring down God's power for a person. My friend cannot go into battles herself anymore, but she can intercede for me on the front lines and play a decisive part in whether we win or lose.

Maybe you are restricted in some way in your ability to get out and teach, preach, witness, or organize, or maybe you have a spiritual inferiority complex because you don't have an obvious ministry gift. Well, Joshua was a great general, but his battlefield exploits did not determine the outcome of the war. The man praying on the hill did. And that's a ministry no one can stop you from having. Prayer does not depend on health, gifts, charisma, money, or influence, and it happens to be the most important ministry of all. You may not feel as if you are doing anything, but you are neutralizing the forces of hell with the power of God.

When it comes to the work of God, you can do the most essential work without ever leaving home. Take your position with Moses of old on that hill of intercession. The warrior on the field will win as long as the prayer warrior is fighting in the throne room.

Kevin Shea was a New York firefighter from Fire Department Rescue Company Number One. It was about 12:20 on a Friday afternoon, and his company got a call to the World Trade Center, those famous twin towers in lower Manhattan. I don't think his crew fully realized what had happened that day. A bomb blast ripped through the basement of the World Trade Center, killing six people. It injured more than a thousand people, emptied out those buildings, and ripped a hole a hundred feet across and three stories deep. A few minutes after the explosion, Kevin Shea and his fire company pulled up. He had already been decorated for heroism in the line of duty, and he was now inching his way across the parking garage of the World Trade Center. Suddenly, the concrete beneath him gave way, and he fell four floors into this crater left by the bomb. His partner saw it, and as he looked into the crater, he just saw roaring flames down there. He said, "I saw his feet, and it looked like he was falling into hell." There is only one reason Kevin Shea didn't die that day. Let's take a God-moment about . . .

Reaching through the Flames

That day, firefighter Kevin Shea landed on a pile of office room dividers, which broke his fall as well as his left knee and foot. In the fall, he lost his helmet and his facemask. The flames were coming his way, and later he said, "Rocks and cinders were falling everywhere, and I thought this is it, and I prayed to God just to take me quick." But Lieutenant Joe Ward lowered himself right into that fiery crater, and by the glow of the flames, he found Kevin Shea, reached out a hand to rescue him, and hoisted him to safety. Someone came to where he was, faced his fire, and brought him back.

That is what the Son of God did for us. Our word from the Word of God comes from Isaiah 53, beginning at verse 5.

Speaking of Christ, the prophet writes, "He was pierced for our transgressions, he was crushed for our iniquities; the punishment that brought us peace was upon him, and by his wounds we are healed. We all, like sheep, have gone astray, each of us has turned to his own way; and the LORD has laid on him the iniquity of us all."

The Bible makes it clear that, like sheep that are away from their shepherd, we are away from God. Every one of us has turned to our own way, the Bible says. Romans 6:23 says that there is a death penalty for that. "The wages of sin is death." Literally, we are falling into hell. No matter how good a person I have been, I have run my own life. I have a sin bill, and no way to pay it. No religion can ever pay it. The only way to pay it is to be away from God forever, and that's hell. But wait, someone is coming in your direction through the fire. It is God's only Son. He knows we will never make it to Him, so He comes to us and our world. He says, "Father, I will face Ron's fire." Put your name in there. "I will face _____'s fire." He takes our hell as He dies on the cross. The punishment that brought us peace was upon Him, and He died so you don't ever have to die spiritually.

Listen to the voice of Jesus reaching through the flames, offering His hand to you. "God so loved the world that he gave his one and only Son, that whoever believes in him shall not perish but have eternal life" (John 3:16). Believe—that is what that fallen firefighter did that day. The Bible says, grab the rescuer if He is your only hope. You could do that right now and say, "Lord, I'm sorry for my sin. I turn from my sin. I'm pinning all my hopes on You and what You did on the cross to have my sin forgiven." You could do that right where you are. Please, don't reject the hand of the One who loves you enough to face your fire so you don't have to.

I am a New York Yankees baseball fan. Now, if you are a Yankees fan, you are not a Toronto Blue Jays fan because there is usually a good pennant race going on between them. In fact, the Blue Jays are the first team ever to take the championship to Canada. The rivalry is okay, but at one particular game that rivalry went too far. With two countries at this game, there were two national anthems played. Someone from the Metropolitan Opera got up to sing "O, Canada," the Canadian national anthem. Some people in the bleachers started to boo during that national anthem. But suddenly, a wave of cheering and applause broke out, and it continued throughout the Canadian anthem. Soon, the good guys who were cheering were making so much noise that it drowned out the booing of the bad guys! Let's take a God-moment about . . .

The Silence of the Good Guys

Our word from the Word of God comes from Psalm 107:1–2. "Give thanks to the LORD, for he is good; his love endures forever. Let the redeemed of the LORD say this—those he redeemed from the hand of the foe." The King James Version says, "Let the redeemed of the LORD say so." This is a call to God's people to make some noise.

The guys in the bleachers sure make their negative noises in our world, whether we're at work, school, the gym, the barbershop, or the beauty shop. People have no shame about sin, about what breaks God's heart. They talk about the raunchy things that went on at a party, what someone did when they drank too much, sexual escapades, a dirty joke, a dirty movie, or the latest scandal. If you judged only by what is talked about most, you would conclude that virtually everyone thinks sin is cool and that what God calls abnormal is really normal. No one seems to care about what is pure, what is right, or what pleases God.

These people are not speaking for us. They are like those bleacher boo-birds—they don't express how most of us feel, but since they are the only ones making noise, it sounds like that's how everyone feels. What we need are people like those who decided to cheer, people who will speak up for what is right. And it needs to be us.

Maybe you have just been sitting by silently, even wincing inside as the people on the road to death are bragging, entertaining, mocking, and promoting the darkness. Everyone

---

Those guys in the stands didn't boo the people who were doing the booing, they just started to make some positive noise to drown them out.

---

around thinks, "I guess this is the only way there is." Well it isn't, and you know it. Isn't it time you spoke up? Don't speak up in a harsh, negative, or judgmental way. Don't attack or put down the promoters of the wrong. Those guys in the stands didn't boo the people who were doing the booing, they just started to make some positive noise to drown them out. It's time you came in talking about a weekend that had no regrets, why you are keeping sex special, and why you are proud to be a virgin. Talk about some heroes who stand up for the right. Talk about how you believe marriage is forever, about how Jesus is answering your loneliness, your guilt, and your pain. People have no idea what Jesus is like, or if they do, they have the wrong idea. Why? Because of the silence of the good guys. Why don't you say, "Lord, help me to never again be ashamed of You, not when You loved me enough to die publicly for me."

I'm tired of the noise from the bleachers of sin, aren't you? Because of Jesus, we have so much more to make noise about. Let's start to hear some positive noise from your section. If you start cheering for what is right, I know you will find others starting to cheer with you.

We have taught our kids many life skills over the years. Skills such as how to talk, how to feed themselves, how to study, and how to have good manners. We've taught them how to ride a bike, how to play various sports, and then how to drive. Recently, we reached a new stage of our coaching career—we had to teach them how to get a job, so we reviewed the basics. Shake hands with a firm handshake. Look employers in the eye. Smile. Don't ask about money right away. Dress up a little bit. Don't go in a T-shirt and shorts. Well, it worked, and they all got jobs.

That skill of making a good impression gets more and more important as our responsibilities grow. Some people even hire a company to write a good résumé for them. We get pretty good at analyzing what will impress others until we meet a person who isn't impressed by any wardrobe or résumé. Let's take a God-moment about . . .

Impressing God

Our word from the Word of God is found in Isaiah 66. "This is the one I esteem" (v. 2). Whoa! God's got my attention on this one. Who does the Lord esteem? "He who is humble and contrite in spirit, and trembles at my word." Whoa. The King James Version says, "To this man will I look," and then gives those same three qualities. The Berkeley translation says, "I will look favorably upon that man." This is a description of the person God will bless, God will use, and God will employ in His service.

He lists three key characteristics. First, He looks at people's attitudes toward themselves. What's your attitude toward yourself? God is impressed with those who are not impressed with themselves. When you realize that you're just His creation, everything you've ever done or been is His gift—so you don't seek glory, you don't seek recognition. When you're effective, you don't say, "Hey, ain't I something?" You say, "Isn't He something?!" God is looking for that attitude toward yourself.

Second, He talks about being contrite in spirit. That's your attitude toward sin. The word *contrite* literally means "crushed in your spirit." This means that you are someone whose sin

---

God is impressed with those who are not impressed with themselves.

---

really makes you sad. You deal with it right away. You don't make any attempt to justify it, rationalize it, or cover it. You're very sensitive about disobeying God. God looks favorably on that kind of person—not a sinless person, but someone who is crushed in their spirit when they sin.

Third, your attitude toward Scripture is important. He speaks of someone who "trembles at my word." He is impressed by someone who is impressed by His Word. Do you still deeply feel the promises, challenges, warnings, and examples of God's Word? That's what impresses God. And notice, there is nothing here about activities, appearance, talent, influence, or money. Three sensitivities that people can't really see and don't often value: You're not impressed by yourself, you are depressed about sin, and you are impressed by God's words.

To impress a human employer, you may need to work on your handshake, your wardrobe, or your résumé. But for the Person you really need to impress, you work on your spirit. "To this person I will look," God says. You know what my prayer is for you? That the Lord will see in you someone He can trust.

If your town has a water tank, I'd guess that it probably has the name of your town on it, right? They all say basically the same thing. Now, once I saw two water tanks that got my attention while we were traveling. We were driving through Virginia, when suddenly I looked up and saw two water tanks on a mountain overlooking this town. You can't miss them. Two tanks, and each one has one word on it. One says, "Hot." The other one says, "Cold." Let's take a God-moment about . . .

No Third Choice

Our word from the Word of God comes from Revelation 3:15–16. God is talking to a church in a place called Laodicea, but He could be talking to some of us today. "I know your deeds, that you are neither cold nor hot. I wish you were either one or the other! So, because you are lukewarm—neither hot nor cold—I am about to spit you out of my mouth." That's strong language. And it's kind of disturbing to some of us who might like our Christianity like our oatmeal—not too hot, not too cold. We don't mind getting a little involved, giving a little money, being a little committed. Perhaps we believe the beliefs, sing the songs, pray the prayers, read the Bible sometimes, help out a little, but let's not get carried away. We don't mind getting hot when it comes to sports, business, recreation, or a relationship, but Jesus? Well, lukewarm is okay. But He'd rather have you cold. That's what He just said. "Won't you be clearly one thing or another? Lukewarm I find repulsive." It's like those water tanks. Hot, cold—only two. There was not a third choice.

There is no third choice with following Jesus either. It's hot or cold. In verse 17, Jesus describes these people a little more. "You say, 'I am rich; I have acquired wealth and do not need a thing.' But you do not realize that you are wretched, pitiful, poor, blind and naked." These people look like they have it totally together. It's easy to mistake success, prosperity, or a good image for spiritual health. But God is not fooled, and here is this poignant picture in chapter 3, verse 20. Talking to the church, Jesus says, "Here I am! I stand at the door and knock. If anyone hears my voice and opens the door, I will come in." Jesus has been locked out of His own church! He has been locked out of a life that He purchased with His life. Maybe it's your life. It's time you let Him in and let Him run things.

Frankly, lukewarm Christianity is hardly worth the trouble. It's boring, it's powerless, it's unsatisfying, and you're sitting there saying, "Man, I wonder why this faith is so lifeless. Why bother with it? See ya." Real Christianity is as radical as taking up a cross daily. This is a time for no more holding back. The Word of God says in Romans 12:1, "In view of God's mercy [what Christ did on the cross for us], offer your bodies as living sacrifices [that's hanging onto nothing], holy and pleasing to God—this is your spiritual act of worship."

There are two signs over God's people: hot and cold. Step up to one or the other, will you? When it comes to the Lord Jesus Christ, remember—there is no third choice.

The Relationship You're Restless For

Unleashing Your Relationship with God

ey, let's choose sides"—that was always the process on our playground before any ball game could begin. Maybe you remember going through this. We would pick two captains, and it was always obvious who they were going to be—they were going to be the most athletic. Then there would be ten guys standing around waiting to be picked for a team. Everybody's trying to look athletic. Of course, you could always guess who would be the first chosen. First picked was the great hitter, the great pitcher, the great shooter, or the great runner. You could also guess who would probably be the last ones chosen. I can remember it seemed like an hour sometimes as they started to pick. They'd go down the line, and then finally they'd get to me. My best hope was to be next to last. There's a little dignity left in that. Sometime or another in your life, you've probably waited to be chosen, and it hurts to be unchosen. Well, let's take a God-moment about . . .

"Congratulations! You've Been Chosen!"

Our word from the Word of God comes from Ephesians 1. Look at this behind-the-scenes view from where God sits. "Praise be to the God and Father of our Lord Jesus Christ, who has blessed us in the heavenly realms with every spiritual blessing in Christ. For he chose us in him before the creation of the world to be holy and blameless in his sight. In love he predestined us to be adopted as his sons through Jesus Christ" (vv. 3–5).

Wow! Did you get that? Chosen by God. No waiting through some excruciating process to see if you're good enough. God has had His eye on you since before there was a world. That's hard to grasp, but every once in a while we get an occasional glimpse of it.

I remember when we were trying to buy our home many years ago. We needed five thousand dollars in five days to secure it, and we thought, surely we'd be able to find that. That started on Monday, and by Friday we'd been unable to get enough. We had to have it by noon, and my wife talked to a friend that morning who called and said, "Have you got it yet?" She said, "No, it looks like the Lord may have something else for us." My wife called me at eleven and said, "What do you think?" I said, "I think we still have an hour. Let's not give up yet." Eleven-thirty, and the husband of that lady called and said, "Ron, you need five thousand dollars. Well, forty years ago my dad set aside this little fund that I have not been able to get

---

Wow! Chosen by God. He's even paid for you with the life of His Son. That's how expensive you are.

---

into until now, and I'd like to lend you, interest free, that money until any day you can pay me back." It was five thousand dollars. God had set aside the money for me to buy a house before there was a me.

See, He's had His eye on you in just the same way. You don't know how much you're worth until you realize that God has chosen you. I don't know how chosen or unchosen you've felt in your life. Maybe you've waited to be chosen for sports, for a date, for recognition, or for marriage. Maybe you've even felt passed over when it comes to a home, living in a world that chooses based on beauty, ability, education, and performance. A lot of us are the unchosen—but not when it comes to the only Person who ultimately matters. God, the Father of our Lord Jesus Christ, who has created it all, says, "I want you," based on His unconditional love. And He's even paid for you with the life of His Son. That's how expensive you are.

So no matter who's ignored you or mistreated you, they've been wrong about you. God has chosen you. Since He's a king and you're His child, doesn't that make you a prince or a princess? You don't have to play all those games to get people to like you. You don't have to throw yourself away as if you aren't worth much. You don't have to settle for mediocrity. You don't have to fight for all those earthly crowns and titles. God has had His eye on you since before there was a world, and He sacrificed His most precious possession for you. Congratulations—you've been chosen!

Our youngest son, Brad, was asleep upstairs, and his dog, Missy, was confined to the kitchen. Our daughter, who was visiting, thought it would be fun to play with Missy, so she removed the gate on the kitchen and let her out. But Lisa did not get to play with Missy because that dog took off like a rocket with a guidance system. Missy made a mad dash down the hall and up the stairs, somehow managed to get Brad's door opened, and jumped into his bed. We didn't even know that she knew where Brad was. Somebody said, "Boy, she's a smart dog." Well, she is. She knows exactly where her master is. She goes straight there. Let's take a God-moment about . . .

Pursuing Your Master

Our word from the Word of God comes from Psalm 42. "As the deer pants for streams of water, so my soul pants for you, O God. My soul thirsts for God, for the living God." David next asks what I think is probably one of the best questions in the Bible: "When can I go and meet with God?" If you are a follower of Christ, you have an instinct to say, "I want to go wherever my Master is and be with Him. As soon as I get a chance, I want to be in His presence." Perhaps, though, this might be what is missing in our relationship with the Lord.

We run to serve Him, to give to Him, to believe in Him, to obey Him, but that's not what David is talking about. David is speaking of a deep passion to be with Him, to be together. And it is motivated by only one thing—a deep love for the Lord. Maybe the most important question Jesus ever asked was, "Do you love Me?" The church at Ephesus in Revelation 2 had it all. They were working hard, they had the right beliefs, but Jesus said, "I hold this against you: You have forsaken your first love" (v. 4).

We are some of the busiest Christians in history. Our church bulletins show we are more Martha running around than Mary sitting at Jesus' feet. Jesus is looking for a heart that loves to be with Him, that pursues Him, and that sets aside time to enjoy

His presence. What might be missing from our active but often unsatisfying faith is simply loving Jesus. As you review each twenty-four hours, look at all He did for you and make your thank you list. Mentally, visit the cross each day and again see what He has done to pay for you.

What might be missing from our active but often unsatisfying faith is simply loving Jesus.

I know Lisa and Rick, our daughter and son-in-law, fell in love when they had an eighteen-hour trip on an airplane on a missions trip. They had focused time together. You will never have that kind of love with Jesus unless you schedule it. Reserve time for the two of you. The old saints used to call this a heart for God, and that is what a relationship with Him is all about. I have watched a little dog live for the moment she can be with her master, run to him whenever there is the smallest opportunity, and find her security and happiness in the time she can be with him. Jesus Christ, God's one and only Son, is *your* master. Be someone who devotedly pursues your Master.

I've noticed that while my car moves slowly through the sprays and brushes of the local car wash, I have plenty of time to talk to the man at the cash register and look at all the car gadgets on the walls. I think they move the car slowly so I'll have plenty of time to buy little things I don't really need. One entire wall at the car wash is covered with a whole display of air fresheners. Now, the only air freshener scents I know of are pine and extra pine, but here there are probably sixty fragrances to choose from! One of them is really amusing. It's called "New Car" air freshener. Yes, you can purchase the scent of a new car. If you have a tired old vehicle with tired old smells to match, you can get this freshener and maybe fool everybody. At least your car will smell new. Let's take a God-moment about how . . .

"New" Is More Than a Smell

Our word from the Word of God comes from Matthew 7, beginning at verse 21. This is one of the most sobering passages in the Bible. Jesus says, "Not everyone who says to me, 'Lord, Lord,' will enter the kingdom of heaven, but only he who does the will of my Father who is in heaven. Many will say to me on that day, 'Lord, Lord, did we not prophesy in your name, and in your name drive out demons and perform many miracles?' Then I will tell them plainly, 'I never knew you. Away from me, you evildoers!'" Wow! These people must have had the fragrance of a Christian, but Jesus says He doesn't know them. He is saying here that it is possible to look very Christian on the outside, even to be in significant Christian leadership, but to somehow miss Jesus—and miss heaven. It is easy to fall into a faith that is in our heads but never gets to our hearts. We can have the Christian vocabulary, a Christian image, a Christian schedule, Christian habits, and all the aromas of someone who really knows Christ. But somehow, we can miss the one transaction that really makes us God's. Jesus says we have to do the will of His Father who is in heaven, and He defined that in John 6:40. "My Father's will is that everyone who looks to the Son and believes in him shall have eternal life." That means we have to pin all our hopes on Jesus Christ. When we look to Him and believe in Him, in a biblical sense we have grabbed Him and said, "Lord, I'm depending totally on You."

There are Christian youth group leaders who have not done that. There are Christian college students who have all the names for all the Christian stuff, but they have never been to the cross to have their own sins forgiven. There are Christian teachers, pastors, and many people who smell new, but it is still the same old person inside. Jesus has never been invited in. Could it be that you are serving Jesus but have never surrendered to Him? I know it is hard to face, but it's harder not to face it. Those awful words, "I never knew you." I never want you to hear those words from Jesus. None of the spiritual decorations or activities impress Him. He knows whether or not there was ever a moment when you really surrendered yourself to Him. When was it? If you are not sure that you've done that, why not do it now? Let Jesus make you really new, inside and out.

Once on an airplane flight from Chicago to Newark, I was busily working when suddenly the pilot put on the brakes. We were not really near Newark yet, so I tried to figure out what was going on. It looked as if the plane was beginning to circle, and our wing was dipped down a little bit. Pretty soon, I said, "You know what? I believe I have seen that house before, that field before, and those trees before." I saw them again, and again, and another time. Yes, we were in that time warp that is dreaded by every frequent flier—the holding pattern. Now, we weren't standing still, but we were using up time and fuel, and we were in constant motion. And we weren't making any progress. Let's take a God-moment about being . . .

Stuck in a Holding Pattern

Our word from the Word of God comes from Philippians 3, beginning at verse 12. Paul says, "Not that I have already obtained all this, or have already been made perfect, but I press on to take hold of that for which Christ Jesus took hold of me. Brothers, I do not consider myself yet to have taken hold of it. But one thing I do: Forgetting what is behind and straining toward what is ahead, I press on toward the goal to win the prize for which God has called me heavenward in Christ Jesus."

If anyone could have been satisfied with where he was spiritually, it would have been the apostle Paul. He was living one of the greatest Christian lives in history. But you can tell from this passage that he is refusing to stay in spiritual neutral. And he certainly wouldn't go in reverse and live on his spiritual memories, going through his scrapbook saying, "Remember the wonderful times the Lord and I had together?" No, Paul is in high gear. He says, "I am pressing on. I haven't got it all yet. I want the rest of Jesus."

Paul never flew, but I don't think he would have liked a holding pattern. Maybe you are in a holding pattern spiritually. You started on your journey in Jesus and made some progress, but somewhere along the way you slowed down, and now you're circling ground you've covered before. You are using up fuel and time in this cycle of sameness. You're going to the meetings, you're giving, you're serving, and you're singing, but it is meaningless motion—a holding pattern. Churches get in holding patterns too. They keep the calendar packed—time for the banquet, time for this activity, time for the board, time for the committee—but are they taking any new ground for the Lord?

Spiritually healthy people are restless people. They are aggressively pursuing more of God's power in their lives than they have ever tasted before. They want a more intimate relationship with Jesus than they have experienced yet. They desire a greater effectiveness in praying than they have had before. They seek to make more of a difference than ever. Is that you? Is that the group you are in? Does that describe your church? Let it begin with you breaking out of your holding pattern and getting moving again. It begins when you say, "Lord, I'm tired of this plateau. Activity is not obedience. I know that. Busyness is not power. I want all You have." Find some others who feel the same way, and pursue the Lord together in a prayer meeting. Make it a discipline to find new ground in God's Word to give Him daily.

Circling the same ground in that airplane, I was restless to get on toward the goal. It was a great feeling when we finally started moving again in the right direction. Aren't you tired of being in a spiritual holding pattern?

He is rapidly becoming one of the most famous rabbits in America. And there are not that many famous rabbits in America. There's Bugs Bunny, Peter Cottontail, and Roger Rabbit, but this one is the new kid on the block. In the middle of a commercial, he will come marching across the screen, beating his drum energetically, drumsticks flying in the air. He's the Energizer Bunny, advertising batteries that supposedly keep "going and going and going . . ." Let's take a God-moment about . . .

Energizer Christians

Our word from the Word of God comes from Luke 9:23. It is a verse for Christians who would like to have the word *consistent* describe their experience in Christ. That's not how we live a lot of our Christian life, is it? We tend to have these spiritual highs. We tend to be roller-coaster Christians. We get this surge of power from this big battery. We go to a meeting, a concert, a retreat, hear a great speaker, or find something that touches us on the radio. We get the surge, and there's a spurt of spiritual victory, but then suddenly we're standing still or falling over. Well, maybe you're tired of brief seasons of excellence with long stretches of spiritual mediocrity in between—up and down, up and down. You're ready to be an energizer Christian—you're ready for Luke 9:23. Here it is, and look for the *D* word. "Then he said to them all: 'If anyone would come after me, he must deny himself and take up his cross daily and follow me.'"

Jesus said, if we want to successfully follow Him, we have to say no to controlling our own lives, and yes to keeping in step with Him. Did you notice the *D* word that is usually missing from our vocabulary? *Daily.* How often should we dedicate our lives? Annually? Semiannually? At the conference? No, daily. This kind of Christian is steady and lives for Jesus one day at a time. It's a twenty-four-hour exercise, as if we will have no other days. I don't think we live the Christian life so much as the Christian day. This is a surrender to Christ that is renewable every morning.

Did you meet with Him this morning? Make sure you've listened to His voice before you listen to any other. As you read His Word, look for some specific part of your life you can

---

> ## *I don't think we live the Christian life so much as the Christian day. This is a surrender to Christ that is renewable every morning.*

---

apply that verse to and give Him that ground for the day. This is an act of specific lordship. "Now, Lord, I know You're the Lord of everything, but today I'm making You the Lord of my impatience toward Bernice. I'm going to make You the Lord of my sarcastic tongue when I'm in these family arguments." Make it whatever you want to give Him. He is the specific Lord of something. I'm talking about a measurable surrender. Then, that night at the end of that "daily," do a personal checkup. Did He change something? Did Jesus touch a real part of you that day? Tomorrow, start with Jesus again.

Now each week is seven new starts with Jesus, so you can never say, "I have dedicated my life." All you can ever say is, "I am dedicating," and He will make those days into weeks and months and years, and a life, and you will keep going and going and going . . .

My friend Rob makes a living selling novelty items. Yes, you can live off of that! People buy novelty items. I confess that I bought one of those terminator things. Did you ever see those little black plastic things that have three buttons on them, and each button makes a different sound? I don't know why I bought it. One of the sounds is a machine gun. If I get impatient with the guys in front of me, I can just press this and it will make a machine gun sound. It also has a death ray sound, so I can try to dematerialize the car that's driving so slowly in front of me.

Remember other novelties like pet rocks? That was big for awhile. There were also the deeley-bobber antennas people would put on their heads, and they would wave back and forth.

Well, there is a clever new novelty item selling at toy shows right now. A company has made two hand-mirrors that make sounds. One mirror shrieks when you look into it, while the other one laughs hysterically. That's just what we need—a mirror with a reaction, right? Maybe the idea isn't all that bad. Let's take a God-moment about . . .

Your Sometimes-Shrieking, Sometimes-Laughing Mirror

Our word from the Word of God comes from the first chapter of James, beginning with verse 22. "Do not merely listen to the word, and so deceive yourselves. Do what it says. Anyone who listens to the word but does not do what it says is like a man who looks at his face in a mirror and, after looking at himself, goes away and immediately forgets what he looks like. But the man who looks intently into the perfect law that gives freedom, and continues to do this, not forgetting what he has heard, but doing it—he will be blessed in what he does."

Here's a pretty radical idea. Every time we read the Bible, something should change. The Bible says that if all we do is read the Bible, we deceive ourselves. We are supposed to change because of the Bible. Isn't that what happens when we look in the mirror in the morning? We get up and say, "I can't believe how much damage six hours can do." Usually, we comb, cover, mousse, or do something before we start the day. The idea behind looking in a mirror is to see what needs changing. That is also the idea behind looking in the Bible.

Like those novelty mirrors, the mirror of God's Word can sometimes make us shriek at what we find, and sometimes it will lighten us up and make us laugh. When we look into God's Word and let it be a mirror, sometimes we'll say, "That's a scary part of my life. What sinful part of me should Jesus and I be working on today?" After looking in the Bible and seeing a God's-eye view of something big and scary, sometimes we'll laugh and say, "That's not so scary. It's big to me, but it's small to my Lord." We can walk away from the Bible feeling lighter because of our new perspective.

You should be different after looking in a mirror, and especially after looking in the Bible mirror. Look in the mirror and say, "How do I look to You today, God?" Walk away cleaner because you dealt with your sin, or lighter because you saw your problem as God sees it. Make sure you act after you look in the mirror of God's Word.

Busy is not a new development in Karen's life or my life. From the time we were newlyweds, we both worked and had a lot of unscheduled ministry hours, as well as after-hours kinds of things when people needed us. So whenever we had any time available, we'd race around trying to get our personal stuff done. Well, on one of those days, Karen went to the local shopping center, racing the clock as we have been all these years, and as she was dashing into the store she realized, "Oh, no, I locked my keys in the car"—with the car still running. Did you ever do that? She tried the time-honored clothes hanger method, all contorted trying to get in the car. It was comforting, at least, to know that our lock was virtually impossible to unlock with a hanger. This car is really secure. Meanwhile, it's still running. That's when the policeman pulled up. My wife said, "Hey, could you help me?" He stood there for a minute, and he said, "Why don't you just go inside, grab your package, and I'll take care of it?" It was obvious to her that he did not want to show her the tricks of breaking into a car. So when she returned just a few moments later, bingo! The car was unlocked. It was amazing how fast he could work when she got out of the way. Let's take a God-moment about . . .

Getting Out of the Way

Our word from the Word of God comes from 2 Chronicles 20, from the days of King Jehoshaphat. It says that he prayed when a great army came against him, "O LORD, God of our fathers, are you not the God who is in heaven? You rule over all the kingdoms of the nations. Power and might are in your hand, and no one can withstand you" (v. 6). In verse 12 he says, "O our God, will you not judge them? For we have no power to face this vast army that is attacking us." Have you ever felt like that? "I do not know what to do, but my eyes are on You." In verse 15 the Lord answers, "Do not be afraid or discouraged because of this vast army. For the battle is not yours, but God's." It's as if God was saying in those days, and maybe to us today, "Get out of the way, and watch what I can do."

Maybe you're trying to fix your own situation right now, and you have your clothes hanger in there, twisting, trying to grab it, and going through all kinds of contortions to unlock things, but all you're getting is frustrated. You say, "Well, I'm seeking God's help," and that's what these verses say. The people of Judah went to seek *help* from the Lord, but instead, they got a total *takeover* from the Lord—and that's what you need right now. You don't need God's *help,* you need God's total control and His total takeover of this vast army situation that's coming against you. You've been keeping one hand on it, trying to protect it, change it, or manipulate it. Could you just surrender and let the Lord have it?

Popular author and college president Jay Kesler says, "The problem with living sacrifices is that they keep crawling off the altar." Maybe that's what you've been doing. Powerful people, resourceful people, strong people, all have a hard time experiencing the full power of God. But Jehoshaphat, the king in his land, says, "O Lord." He's just desperate. He does this intense praying. There's this deep surrender. He says, "Lord, I have no power. I can't contribute to the solution at all." He says, "It's total trust. We have our eyes only on You."

Well, maybe there's a vast army against you right now, and given the odds, it's a defeat for you. But if it's a vast army against God, the victory is coming. Why don't you say, "Lord, I give up my cleverness, my experience, my persuasion, my nagging, my scheming, my promoting. It's not my battle anymore." In moments, that policeman unlocked what my wife had not been able to unlock with all her best efforts—but she had to get out of the way, and so do you. God is standing by, not to help, but to take over. Why don't you move over and see what He can do!

Every once in a while, comic strips really have something to say. Have you ever seen "B. C."? He is this little scraggly haired caveman that makes some fairly modern observations. I think the best one appeared one Easter. Here is B. C., outside a tomb with a rock next to it. Then, in the next panel, he goes in the tomb and looks around. In the third panel, he finds the tomb empty. Finally, in the last panel, he comes out, stands outside the empty tomb, and shouts one word: "Yes!" Let's take a God-moment about . . .

A Place to Say "Yes!"

Our word from the Word of God comes from Acts 2, and actually, I could divide what I'm going to say into three "panels": a hill, a hole, and a heart. Peter is preaching just weeks after Jesus' crucifixion and resurrection, and some of the people in the crowd were probably among those who had called for His death. So Peter says, "You, with the help of wicked men, put him to death by nailing him to the cross. But God raised him from the dead, freeing him from the agony of death, because it was impossible for death to keep its hold on him" (vv. 23–24). Later on, Peter continues, "Be assured of this: God has made this Jesus, whom you crucified, both Lord and Christ" (v. 36). The reaction? "When the people heard this, they were cut to the heart and said to Peter and the other apostles, 'Brothers, what shall we do?'" (v. 37).

Centuries have passed, but Peter's message is the same for your life and mine. A hill comes first, the hill of Calvary. I invite you to walk up to the top of that hill where the cross is and look into the face of Jesus there. The Bible says that you have crucified Him, and actually, we all did. He didn't go there because Roman soldiers or Jewish leaders made Him go there. Jesus died on the cross because it was the only way to pay the death penalty for your sin and mine. Have you ever walked up to that hill and up to the cross and said, "For me. This is for me"? In Galatians 2:20, Paul says, "The life I live in the body,

THE RELATIONSHIP YOU'RE RESTLESS FOR

I live by faith in the Son of God, who loved me and gave himself for me." That's the hill.

Now, there's a hole. It's the hole where Jesus was buried, and nobody's there. Jesus blew the doors off His grave that Easter morning; it was impossible for death to keep its hold on Him. Only one person can give you unending and uninterrupted

---

> ### *Only one person can give you unending and uninterrupted life. That's the Man who has it Himself, the Man who conquered death.*

---

life. That's the Man who has it Himself, the Man who conquered death. Stand at that hole in the ground, at that empty tomb where Jesus is no more, and say, "For sure. This thing is for sure." This is not blind faith or religious dogma. You know a living Savior . . . or you can know Him.

Then there's a heart. Scripture says that the people were cut to the heart by what they heard and asked, "What shall we do?" I hope that is your question today. If Jesus has been on that cross for me, if He blew the doors off death, and if He has eternal life to offer, what shall I do? The answer is to say "Yes!" Say yes to Jesus. You may have a head full of Christian facts, a checkbook full of Christian contributions, a calendar full of Christian meetings, but a heart still empty of Jesus. When Thomas saw this living Jesus, he fell at His feet and said, "My Lord and my God!" Isn't it time for you to say, "My Lord! My God! My Savior!"? Walk up that hill where the cross is and say, "For me." Come by the victory of the empty tomb and say, "For sure." And make today the day you come to Jesus and say, "Yes!"

Over the years, my kids haven't really been too interested in my upcoming speaking engagements, with one exception. My boys have always asked if I was doing pro sports chapels. Occasionally, when the guys were little, they would go with me. It was wonderful to take them along, but there were some rules. I told them they couldn't act impressed by the players, because chapel is their personal time, and athletes are appropriately sensitive. They don't want to be celebrities giving out autographs at their church and mealtime. So I told my kids, "Guys, if you want to continue to have this privilege, you need to be cool when you're there." My one son Brad would be cool on the outside, acting as if he was eating breakfast next to any man on the street instead of some sports hero, but when he got to the car, he yelled, "Yeeaahhhh!" He had been very impressed by whom he was with and stifling a "Wow!" the whole time. Let's take a God-moment about . . .

An Appropriate "Wow!"

Our word from the Word of God comes from Isaiah 6, beginning at verse 1. "I saw the Lord seated on a throne, high and exalted, and the train of his robe filled the temple. Above him were seraphs, each with six wings: With two wings they covered their faces, with two they covered their feet, and with two they were flying. And they were calling to one another: 'Holy, holy, holy is the LORD Almighty; the whole earth is full of his glory.' At the sound of their voices the doorposts and thresholds shook and the temple was filled with smoke. 'Woe to me!' I cried. 'I am ruined! For I am a man of unclean lips, and I live among a people of unclean lips, and my eyes have seen the King, the LORD Almighty.'" Can you feel Isaiah's awe and wonder? He shows us what it is like to be in the presence of God. One word would describe it—wow! Like Brad, Isaiah was very impressed by whom he was with. On a much higher level, that is how we are supposed to be when we pray—very impressed by whom we are with, but not stifling the "Wow!"

At Mount Palomar, they will tell you they have discovered 100 billion galaxies. Prayer is consciously entering the throne room from which 100 billion galaxies are governed. Wow! Do you know whom you are with when you pray? Do you know

---

Prayer is consciously entering the throne room from which 100 billion galaxies are governed. Wow! Prayer will never again be boring or mundane.

---

where you are? It will change how you pray. Prayer will never again be boring or mundane. You will pray humbly, deeply, dependently, understanding whom you are with, laying aside your little powerless power for His unlimited power. You will pray boldly.

When you pray to this God, knowing that you are in the throne room, pray for supernatural things that only God could do. God-sized things. Pray passionately, overwhelmed not by your problem but by God's majesty and love. The One who is totally in charge is totally committed to you. When you pray, make sure you consciously enter the throne room from which the galaxies are governed. Maybe the first word we ought to say when we pray is "Wow!"

My friend Timmy is discovering the world. He doesn't get around so well, and he mostly uses his hands to explore his world. Just months old, Timmy is adorable with chubby cheeks, a shock of light brown hair, and big blue eyes. When Diane brought her new son to our house for the first time, my wife, Karen, had Timmy in her arms almost immediately. Of course, Timmy started exploring. His hands reached for Karen's face. Those little hands touched her cheek, her nose, her chin, and her eyelid, and I heard Karen say, "Look! He's touching my face. He's trying to get to know me." Let's take a God-moment about . . .

The Face of Intimacy

Our word from the Word of God comes from 1 Chronicles 16:11. If we could make a lifestyle of these few simple words, we could experience a closeness to God our hearts have always hungered for. God's Word gives us this urging: "Look to the LORD and his strength; seek his face always." In God's formula for spiritual revival, He directs His people to "humble themselves and pray and seek my face" (2 Chron. 7:14). These commands leap to life when you watch a little baby like Timmy "seeking someone's face."

When God says, "Seek my face," He is inviting us to intimate knowing. He says, "Come really close." The problem is, we don't seek His face to get to know Him. We seek His hands. We say, "God, I need You to do something for me." We seek His head and say, "Lord, I want to know about You. I seek Your brain." After we are Christians for awhile, we begin to just accumulate spiritual knowledge.

The Lord wants us to sit next to Him just because we want to be with Him. He is looking for us to seek His face and to have some no-agenda time with Him. When is the last time you did that? Thank Him for His character, His personality,

His generosity, and His treatment of you. Listen for His leading. Practice His presence in your time alone.

Maybe you have been around your Lord. Maybe you have been learning about your Lord. Maybe you have been doing

---

When God says, "Seek my face,"
He is inviting us
to intimate knowing.
He says, "Come really close."

---

things for your Lord, but you are not with Him much. Let your Father pick you up at least once a day and hold you close. Reach out and seek His face. Then maybe God might say about you, "Hey, look! He's touching My face. He's trying to get to know Me."

Certain occupations require a particularly strong self-image. For example, a dentist needs a strong self-image. Here is a real professional helping people, but everyone dreads what you do. You also probably need a pretty strong self-image to be an IRS agent. Or how about a baseball umpire? Everybody thinks they can see better than you can, yelling, "Hey, are you blind?" because they don't agree with your call. Fans comment on the intelligence of the umpire when they disagree, but you cannot have baseball without umpires. Imagine the players trying to agree on whether a guy was safe or out at second. That would end the game right there! How about letting the fans decide? There would be chaos without the umpire. Thousands of voices may give their opinion about whether the runner was safe or not, but there's only one voice that matters. The umpire settles it. Let's take a God-moment about . . .

Your Own Personal Umpire

Our word from the Word of God comes from Colossians 3:15. God says, "Let the peace of Christ rule in your hearts, since as members of one body you were called to peace." Notice, it says the peace of Christ should *rule* in your hearts. In the original language of the New Testament, that word means to be the judge, the one who awards the prize. In essence, let the peace of Christ be the umpire in our hearts. As we make each day's choices, we need some way to decide what should be safe and what should be out. The Bible says, "Let the peace of Christ decide."

Now, this peace comes as we bring a choice to God. We come to Him with a blank piece of paper and say, "God, You know what I would like, but I'm not going to give You a contract to sign. This is my blank piece of paper. What do *You* want?" As we pray it through, we will find that one way or one road feels right most of the time. I am not talking about rushed prayer here. We must have time to let God put His thoughts into our hearts.

Now, as we get off our knees and start to go through the day, the peace of Christ is going to be challenged by lots of other voices, like the umpire challenged by all those people in the stands. God's will starts to seem a little less clear. How can

---

The more we are full of God's Word, the more material God has to work with in giving us His personal guidance. His peace and His Word always go together.

---

we tune our "peace meter" to hear and receive the peace of Christ? The next verse says, "Let the word of Christ dwell in you richly." We need to have some increased time in God's Word. We need to memorize some verses. We need to read whenever we can, looking for a personal word from the Lord. The more we are full of God's Word, the more material God has to work with in giving us His personal guidance. His peace and His Word always go together.

Human umpires are right some of the time, but God's umpire is right all the time. Offer your choices to the Lord, and ask for His peace as the confirming signal in your heart. Listen to that sense you have of a divine okay or a divine forget it. God's peace is His wonderful way of calling safe or out, and you will always win if you go along with your personal umpire.

It's true, I am a city boy. But for two years, I did live on a farm. When you live on the farm, the rites of manhood include pheasant hunting in the fall. So my dad stuck a twelve-gauge shotgun in my hand and said, "We're going pheasant hunting with all the other men." Now, I had to know what to do with that twelve-gauge shotgun, so I practiced a little bit, then I headed out with all the *men* into the cornfield. I still remember that morning. I was sort of hoping I would find a pheasant, and sort of hoping I wouldn't. Well, wouldn't you know, there was a rustling in the corn row right in front of me, and this pheasant started fluttering around and began taking flight. I fumbled around with the gun, trying to put it up against my shoulder. I wasn't sure which one of us was more scared. There I was at the moment of truth, struggling through the three steps to hitting your target. You have to have your gun loaded and ready, and I did. You have to have your target in sight, and I did. And of course, you have to pull the trigger. Let's take a God-moment about . . .

Nothing without the Trigger

Our word from the Word of God comes from Matthew 9, beginning at verse 20, where Jesus is involved in a miraculous healing. "Just then a woman who had been subject to bleeding for twelve years came up behind him and touched the edge of his cloak. She said to herself, 'If I only touch his cloak, I will be healed.'" But Jesus turned and saw her, and He said, "'Take heart, daughter, your faith has healed you.' And the woman was healed from that moment." A little later in the chapter, probably in the same day, Jesus "went on from there, [and] two blind men followed him, calling out, 'Have mercy on us, Son of David!' When he had gone indoors, the blind men came to him, and he asked them, 'Do you believe that I am able to do this?' 'Yes, Lord,' they replied. Then he touched their eyes and said, 'According to your faith will it be done to you'; and their sight was restored" (vv. 27–30).

Let's talk about the hunt you're on right now—the hunt for that answer you really need, the breakthrough that you've been hoping and praying for, that miracle you really need right now. You have your target in sight. For the bleeding woman, it was her illness; for the blind men, their sight. Maybe for you it's a hopeless medical situation. Maybe your target is a marital problem, or a child or parent who concerns you. Maybe it's a financial impossibility. You know what it is. Now, your gun is loaded, the gun that could bring down what you need. You know what the gun is? The power of God to change that situation. He could do in a moment what human beings couldn't do in twelve years. You need to get the bullet of God's intervening power to the target of that human impossibility. Here you are at the moment of truth.

Well, I didn't come home with a pheasant that day. Do you know why? I didn't pull the trigger. Now, that might be what's standing between you and your personal miracle. The trigger of the supernatural is faith—acting as if God is going to intervene. Not just talking to the Lord about it, but trusting Him to do something supernatural to make the difference, and then acting as if He will. "According to your faith will it be done to you," Jesus promised the blind men. "Your faith has healed you," He reassured the bleeding woman. All through the Bible it's like that. Jesus responds to this kind of active, forward-gear kind of faith, not passive, noncommittal faith. Jesus responds to trust that moves boldly, courageously, and expectantly, even patiently when needed.

Picture it. Here's your rifle, loaded with the bullet of the Lord's intervening power. Aim it at the target of your human impossibility. Now pull the trigger—exercise the faith that delivers God's power to your problem. Your Lord will pierce your need, within the boundaries of His will. He will do as much as you trust Him to do.

ake up kids!" It was 3:30 in the morning. I didn't want to wake up the whole campground, but I did want the kids up in the middle of the night. You ask, "What are you doing to your kids?" Well, I had planned a trip up Cadillac Mountain, and it takes about an hour to drive to the top of it. I had been told that it was the first place you could see the sunrise on the East Coast, and I thought this would be a great adventure for my wife and kids. Well, they were not quite as enthused as I was, especially when I woke them up. So as they got up, I stuffed a donut in each mouth so they wouldn't wake up the campground. Then we started my well-planned adventure up Cadillac Mountain. We made it to the top, and there on the eastern horizon in that chilly, early morning air, we were rewarded with an unforgettable view . . . of the clouds. I had listened to the weather forecast. They had promised me the sun. I had a family insurrection on my hands. Let's take a God-moment about . . .

Disappointment Mountain

Our word from the Word of God comes from Matthew 6:32–33. Jesus has been talking about clothes, food, and earthly possessions. He says, "The pagans run after all these things, and your heavenly Father knows that you need them. But seek first his kingdom and his righteousness, and all these things will be given to you as well."

Jesus is talking about two mountains. One is Earth-Stuff Mountain, and He says most people who don't know Him are climbing this mountain, saying, "I have to collect as much earth stuff as I can." Then He describes climbing Kingdom Mountain, which is seeking first the kingdom of God.

Even if you are a Christian, unless you make a conscious, courageous choice to climb Kingdom Mountain with your life, you will spend your best years and your best energy on

Mount Earth-Stuff. At a seminar I taught about peaceful living in a stressful world, a successful man in his thirties told me he had come that day to find out how to be more successful. He said, "Ron, I'm an athlete. I've been a winner all my life. I want to learn how to win better in my business." At the end of the day, he walked out in tears. Do you know what he said? "All these years, I have been climbing the wrong mountain, and I want the rest of my life to be in the service of the Lord." Maybe you have been climbing the wrong mountain too. You love Jesus, but you're living for earth stuff. You have all your plans together. You work hard. You're getting to the top. But when you get there, will you say, "Wait a minute! Why am I so empty? This isn't the view I expected"?

The Bible says God has planted eternity in your heart. You are built to live for eternal things. Would you let Jesus challenge your daily value system? Would you let Him loosen your grip on all you have accumulated? Would you let Him evaluate your dreams in the light of eternity? Let Him change what you're aiming your efforts at. He wants to be the Lord of your drive to win, to achieve, to conquer. He doesn't want to remove it. He wants to redirect it to climb a better mountain, one that is worth all you have because the view at the top of Mount Kingdom is all that your soul ever longed for.

When Karen and I are driving somewhere, we don't lose any time when she drives. In fact, we've even set some records! One time I was preparing for the meetings we were going to while she drove down this four lane, divided highway. All of a sudden, I looked up and saw orange plastic cones on the middle line that divides the two lanes on our side. Every vehicle but one was moving to the left of the cones. I said every car but one, and that was us. Karen continued in the right lane, and I said, "Honey, what are you doing? It looks like this lane is closing." She said, "Just watch." We passed the line of cars on our left with a big truck at the head of it. See, that truck had moved into the left lane, and all the other drivers had thought, "Oh, that must be the lane to be in," and followed it. But that truck was only taking equipment to a big tar truck parked in the left lane, so we waved as we zipped by all those cars headed for an unpleasant surprise. Let's take a God-moment about . . .

Looking Good, Going Nowhere

Our word from the Word of God comes from Proverbs 14:12. It's short, but it's hard-hitting. "There is a way that seems right to a man, but in the end it leads to death." Well, the Bible is pretty clear here. A lot of people are on a road that looks good, but it's going nowhere. Well, actually, it's going to death. Jesus talked more about that in Matthew 7:13–14 when He said, "Enter through the narrow gate. For wide is the gate and broad is the road that leads to destruction, and many enter through it. But small is the gate and narrow the road that leads to life, and only a few find it." See, lots of people are wrong about the one thing we can't afford to be wrong about . . . how to get to God. If we're wrong about how to get to God, it is eternally fatal. We might be on a sincere road that seems right, but it ends far away from God forever instead of with Him forever. The Bible says many drive on that kind of road, just like those cars following that truck. Almost everybody chose that lane. It seemed like the best one, but it led to an unpleasant end.

Only God can tell us how to get to Him, and He does in John 14:6. Jesus says, "I am the way and the truth and the life. No one comes to the Father except through me." First John 5:11–12 tells us, "God has given us eternal life, and this life is in his Son. He who has the Son has life; he who does not have the Son of God does not have life." Now, it bothers a lot of people that Jesus is the only way. They say, "Well, I believe in tolerance. As long as we're sincere . . ." Well, if you're trapped in a burning building, and a firefighter risks his life to bring you out, I don't think you'd say, "Hey, wait, you mean there's only one way out of here?" No, you grab that rescuer and say, "Thank God there is a way out."

Well, thank God there *is* one way. There wasn't *any* until the Savior came and paid the penalty for our sin—the death penalty. Someone had to die for my sin. No good works—not Christian or Jewish or Muslim or Buddhist or anybody's good works—can pay that death penalty. Romans 5:8 says, "God demonstrates his own love for us in this: While we were still sinners, Christ died for us." If you haven't pinned all your hopes on Jesus the rescuer, you're still on the road that leads to death. There are a lot of wrong ideas about the right way to God, but there's only one way to get there. That's why everything, for now and forever, depends on what you do with God's Son, Jesus. Only one lane gets you to God and gets you to heaven. It's the road that goes by the cross, where Jesus died to pay for your sin. Meet Him there today.

You can get into a pretty good debate among American sports fans over which sport is the most exciting. Now, I think my two sons would vote for basketball as the most exciting sport, and basketball action is pretty physical. I mean, it's constantly changing, it's intense, it's unpredictable. There's only one point where it slows down a little—and much to the relief of the players. You probably know that if a player is fouled by someone from the other team he gets to shoot one or two free throws. That's the one time when nobody's bothering you—there are not all these guys trying to stop you from getting your shot. Actually, I shouldn't say no one is bothering you, especially if you are the visiting team. See, when you're facing the basket, you are also facing all those local fans who want you to miss. They jump up and down, make noise, wave arms, and wave signs. So if you're trying to score some points, you really need to concentrate. Let's take a God-moment about . . .

How to Beat
the Distraction Action

Our word from the Word of God comes from Hebrews 12:1–2. "Since we are surrounded by such a great cloud of witnesses, let us throw off everything that hinders and the sin that so easily entangles, and let us run with perseverance the race marked out for us. Let us fix our eyes on Jesus, the author and perfecter of our faith." This passage suggests a word that's common in modern athletics. You hear this word often: focus. That basketball player has to focus on the basket. That's what it takes to sink it when you have a thousand nuts out there trying to get you to look somewhere else. That player has to tune it all out. His eye is fixed on the basket.

The Bible says we have a race marked out for us. The Lord has set a course for our lives. We have gifts to use for Him, people to influence for Him, work to get done for Him, days with which to glorify Him, and we're like runners striding toward the prize. All that matters is getting to the tape. A runner can look at the crowd, look at the competitors behind, look down, but a champion always focuses on the goal. As you run your lap for Jesus each day, you face plenty of distractions,

---

Frankly, I'm tired of throwing away days to frustration, worry, wandering, self-pity, and panic. What's the answer? Focus.

---

don't you? Problem people, finances, making money, a thousand little annoyances, temptations, an overwhelming to-do list. Maybe you're drawn to a conflict, a fear, or a worry, and it's yelling, "Look over here at me!" Peter's walk on water is a perfect example. As long as he looked at Jesus, he was on top of the storm. When he looked away, it was on top of him. We sink when we look at the storm instead of the Savior.

Frankly, I'm tired of throwing away days to frustration, worry, wandering, self-pity, and panic. What's the answer? Focus. This begins when our day begins. We fill up with Jesus in the early moments. Listen to worship music and Christian radio, take time to hear the Lord in His Word, and then refocus on Him several times during the day. That's why I get a practical benefit from just giving thanks for my meals. We need to determine that we will look for the Lord's hand in our day and thank Him every time we spot Him doing something. We can whisper His name as we answer the phone, answer a letter, answer the door, answer a question. When we feel our old nature taking over, we can think about the cross, about personally being at the cross, about Jesus being worshiped in heaven by a hundred million angels.

Refocus on Jesus. The distracters will always be there, waving, shouting, and screaming for your attention. But a champion knows that distractions don't have to make the difference. Make sure your eyes are stubbornly focused on the Christ who is Lord over every distraction.

I am easily amazed by technology, so I am *totally* amazed by Karen's camera. And she is quite a photographer. She can take the same camera and get two totally different views just by using two different lenses. For example, when she puts on the wide-angle lens, she can get a picture of an entire football field with that camera. And when she changes over to what is called a macro lens, which really magnifies things, she can fill that camera's view with one face in the stands. It amazes me to see how that camera can go from the big picture to the smallest details. Let's take a God-moment about . . .

The Galaxies and the Groceries

Our word from the Word of God comes from Matthew 6:9–11. Jesus says, "This, then, is how you should pray: 'Our Father in heaven, hallowed be your name, your kingdom come, your will be done on earth as it is in heaven. Give us today our daily bread.'" Of course, this is an excerpt from what we know as the Lord's Prayer. This prayer is really a camera with two lenses looking at our heavenly Father. When you hear the word *father,* I don't know what that means to you. I do not know what your father experience was growing up. But I do know that when we think about God being our Father, we are thinking about the father you and I all wish we had.

Now, look at God with the wide-angle lens trained on Him. He is in heaven. His name is to be revered, hallowed, and reverenced, and we should be driven to our knees by who He is. He is the God who rules a hundred billion galaxies, and when we pray, we are in the throne room from which it is all governed. Prayer should never be boring, wimpy, or trivial again when we know whom we are with.

The Lord's Prayer says, "Your kingdom come, your will be done on earth as it is in heaven." Here is God's agenda on earth, His whole cosmic agenda, and the prayer is, "Lord, help me plug into Your cosmic agenda with my life. Your will that is done so awesomely in heaven, we want it done on earth." We should pray with a sense of the bigness and the awesomeness of God.

Then all of a sudden the Lord's Prayer switches lenses. "Give us today our daily bread." Jesus is telling us that we can come to this awesome Father with His incredible eternal plan and even ask Him about today's lunch. Talk about going from the wide-angle to the macro lens! We can aim all the power of heaven on a very real need on earth. Here is this hallowed Father in heaven, who is bringing in a great kingdom and has this tremendous eternal will, and we can talk to Him about our daily bread. Hebrews 4:16 encourages us to "approach the

---

Jesus is telling us that we can come to this awesome Father with His incredible eternal plan and even ask Him about today's lunch.

---

throne of grace with confidence, so that we may receive mercy and find grace to help us in our time of need." This is God through the macro lens. He is the God who cares about the details of your life. He cares about your bank account, about today's little need, about that hard phone call, and about the rent. He cares about the car, the trip, the repairs, the discomfort, and a million other details that make up our days.

What a Father we have, and we can come right to Him with any prayer. What a miracle prayer is—it brings us into the presence and love of a God who is big enough to rule the universe . . . and small enough to care about our groceries.

The airlines know how easily bored we are, so they provide various forms of diversion and entertainment. For example, they hand out headsets on the plane so you can listen to several styles of music, or even to the conversation between the pilot and the tower. If you know your flight number, you can follow the communication that involves your plane. The air traffic controllers clear your pilot for takeoff, and later at another tower, they will clear him for landing. But they also stay in touch all the time *between* the takeoff and the landing. There is more to the flight than just the beginning and the end. The pilot needs to know if there are other planes nearby or of bad weather that demands a change of plans. I'm glad the pilot doesn't turn off the tower after he takes off. Let's take a God-moment about being . . .

Always in Touch with the Tower

Our word from the Word of God comes from Galatians 5:25. God says, "Since we live by the Spirit, let us keep in step with the Spirit." This verse is talking about the internal guidance system we got the day we opened our lives to Jesus as our personal Savior. This system is the Holy Spirit of God, living in our bodies and in our personalities. All day long, He tries to tell us the next thing God wants us to do, avoid, change, or decide. That's why it says "keep in step with the Spirit." We never know where the Lord might want to steer us next.

Now, there is a problem with us busy people. We check in with the tower when we take off in the morning, and then don't usually check in again until the end of the day's flight. As the day heats up, we tend to turn off our radios, take off our headsets, and make a hundred little decisions on our own without consulting the Lord. We get cut off from the tower, so we end up in a lot of turbulence and sometimes get off course. We crash into people. We make unnecessary mistakes. Following Jesus means listening to the Spirit's directing all day long, not just at the beginning and the end.

I am a straight ahead, go for it, make a schedule, make a plan, make a list kind of person, and sometimes I have been so goal oriented that I have turned off the tower. At that point, I cannot hear the inner promptings of the Holy Spirit, so I often miss one of the great gifts I got when I got Jesus—the perfect guidance of my Creator, who makes no mistakes. So I am trying to become a better listener to the Holy Spirit in me, and it is exciting. I encourage you to check in regularly through the day. "Which way do you want to go now, Lord? What should

---

We check in with the tower when we take off in the morning, and then don't usually check in again until the end of the day's flight. Following Jesus means listening to the Spirit's directing all day long, not just at the beginning and the end.

---

come first?" Allow the Spirit to steer you into things and people you never planned. They might look like detours, but if the Spirit pulls you in that direction, it's the right flight plan.

In Acts 16 Paul thought he was supposed to go to Asia Minor. That was his plan A. The Spirit said no, he waited, and the Lord said, "I'm actually taking you to Europe." That was plan B, Paul thought, but it had been God's plan A all along. But Paul understood that obedience requires flexibility—I call it "Spiritinaity." You have to stop and call that person the Lord leads you to call for some unknown reason. He might be leading you to write to someone, to stop for someone, to hug a child, to spend time with someone you love or who needs you, to wait when you want to plunge ahead, or to go for it when you want to wait.

Practice seeking the Lord's prompting, listening to His prompting, and acting on His prompting. That is how you end up on course, living every day in the center of the will of God. If you want the safest route to the best destination, keep your headset on from takeoff to landing every day. Stay in touch with the tower.

One of my responsibilities over the years has been to meet with people who could support ministry financially. I remember when I went to have lunch with a prominent Christian businessman and took Mike, a youth worker, along with me. I wanted him to learn a little bit about how to share the ministry with someone like this. We were in New York City, and much to my surprise, this businessman suggested that we go to his private club. We would have never got past the door without him. Well, there was a problem. At the door, the maître d' turned to Mike and said, "Sorry, sir, you cannot eat here. We require a jacket and tie." Mike had dressed as he usually did—for youth ministry—so he was wearing slacks and a sport shirt. I think they managed to find a jacket and a tie somewhere, but Mike learned that day that in certain situations, casual just isn't appropriate. Let's take a God-moment about how . . .

Casual Is Out

Our word from the Word of God comes from Luke 8, where we'll meet three different people who came to Jesus. Though very different, they all have one thing in common: They all fell at Jesus' feet. The first is a madman who has been taken over by demons. It says in Luke 8, he "had not worn clothes or lived in a house, but had lived in the tombs." Verse 28 says, "When he saw Jesus, he cried out and fell at his feet."

Then in verse 41 we find a different man, "a man named Jairus, a ruler of the synagogue, [who] came and fell at Jesus' feet, pleading with him to come to his house" because his daughter was dying.

Finally in verse 47 we meet a lady who has had a medical problem for twelve years, and she desperately comes to Jesus for a solution. Scripture says, "Then the woman, seeing that she could not go unnoticed, came trembling and fell at his feet." Now, you have a demon enslaved man, the desperate father of a dying girl, and a hopelessly suffering woman, but they're all in the same spot—falling at Jesus' feet.

Modern Christians suffer from a reverence deficit. We are so familiar with Jesus that we are casual in approaching Him. The Bible says we can come boldly, but where is the worship, the reverence, the awe of realizing whom we're with? We're with the King, the Lord, the Creator, the Lamb. Someday every knee will bow at His name. Too often we come to the throne room like Mike came to that restaurant—casual. We cruise into Jesus' presence, sit down, and start talking. But these people in Luke 8, even one who was controlled by demons, knew that the place to be is on the ground when you are in front of Jesus Christ.

The Jesus we come to is the One John portrayed in Revelation. "When I saw him, I fell at his feet as though dead" (1:17). Maybe it's time we move from our seat to our knees—or even facedown on the ground. There is nothing sacred about posture, but our hearts need humility and awe when we pray. We can enter His throne room boldly, we come because of His grace, but let's never forget how awesome this Savior is. Once we allow ourselves to be overwhelmed by Jesus, nothing else is overwhelming. When the great evangelist Gypsy Smith was eighty-two and still preaching, someone asked, "How come you got so much energy?" Maybe his answer should be yours and mine as we get close to Jesus: "I've never lost the wonder."

I am not a rookie at high school graduations. Since I have spent many years in youth ministry, I have been to many of them. I went to our daughter Lisa's graduation from high school, then our son Doug's, but there was something especially tender about Brad's. His was the last graduation in our family that I would be attending. Of course, Brad is now bigger than me, but he is still the baby. I was unusually touched when I heard "Pomp and Circumstance" and he walked across that platform. I thought, "We're on the edge of three new beginnings. Brad is going to start life all over in a brand-new world called college. He and the young lady he has dated during high school are going to different colleges, so their relationship is going to change. And then Karen and I will head into empty-nest time." There was a new beginning for Brad, for his girlfriend, and for his parents. But actually life is all about new beginnings and starting overs, from the day we start kindergarten and leave our parents, to the day we retire, and beyond. I talked to a precious ninety-seven-year-old great-grandmother not long ago. She has seen a lot of new beginnings, and she has great news for every one of us. Let's take a God-moment about . . .

Something Old in Your New Beginning

This grandma said to me that her favorite verse over all these years had been Hebrews 13:8. When she quoted it to me, her face lit up like she was twenty years old again, and she spoke without hesitation. Here is why her smile can light up a room, even though she can't leave that room. "Jesus Christ is the same yesterday and today and forever." Now, this lady is an expert on new beginnings. Her graduation was a long time ago. She has been through romances, the new beginning of marriage, moving several times, new children, her children leaving, grandchildren, and great-grandchildren. She has buried her husband. She is now limited to life in a wheelchair. But one thing has never changed—Jesus Christ, the same yesterday, today, and forever.

Maybe you are facing one of those starting-over times right now. You're entering uncharted territory, and you feel vulnerable, afraid, unprotected, and unsure. Remember, the One who led you in every other place is leading just as steadily now. The One who met your needs before will meet them today. The One who protected you from harm, the other new beginnings, and even from yourself is guarding you just as closely in this time.

I often see billboards for an insurance company that says it is rock solid. Well, there is really only one rock solid. Jesus cannot be touched by recession, inflation, depression, an energy shortage, a bank collapse, illness, or a bomb. If you have turned from your own control of your life and pinned all your hopes on what Jesus did on the cross, you really do have the only thing that is rock solid. You will never enter any situation without the love, leadership, power, and authority of the Son of God. When you face the final graduation, from earth to eternity, you will face the last new beginning—eternity with God or without Him. That graduation all depends on whether you choose Him while you can. For a great-grandmother's ninety-seven years or for every starting over of your life, Jesus Christ is the same yesterday, today, and forever.

The Hard Times That Hurt You

Winning When You're Hurting

Becky was my first serious crush. Serious meaning I thought she was beautiful. At least that's what my thirteen-year-old eyes told me, and that's why I was so surprised when she said she had been in a violent automobile accident not too long before that. She said it had done serious damage to her face, and there were all kinds of scars. Well, I sure couldn't see any trace of them. I know that thirteen-year-old love is blind, but something had obviously happened to those scars. And it did. A plastic surgeon had very skillfully taken them and re-created something beautiful. Let's take a God-moment about . . .

Beautiful Scars

Our word from the Word of God comes from 2 Corinthians 1:3–4. Here is what the apostle Paul says, "Praise be to the God and Father of our Lord Jesus Christ, the Father of compassion and the God of all comfort, who comforts us in all our troubles, so that we can comfort those in any trouble with the comfort we ourselves have received from God." These verses are about something that is common to all of us—the pain of life. I don't know where your pain comes from, whether it's medical or emotional, memories on replay, or something in living color right now, but these verses talk about what the master Plastic Surgeon can make out of the pain of your life. It says here that He turns trouble for us into comfort for others. He is the God of all compassion and the God of all comfort. If we uncover our scars, hurts, and pain to Him, He gives us something to give other people who are hurting. In other words, in God's skillful hands, the ugly can become something beautiful.

Maybe the pain of your life is never far away. Maybe you see scenes on the video replay unit in your mind or maybe it's happening right now. You don't have a choice about having the pain, but you do have two choices about what you do with that hurt.

First, you can turn it inward. That is what most people do. When you turn it inward and continue to work on it, replay it, and think about it, it turns into self-pity, then bitterness and

---

In God's skillful hands, the ugly can become something beautiful.

---

negative attitudes. The ugly becomes uglier. You make the scars deeper. The other option is to turn it outward. This pain can be turned outward in the form of sensitivity and compassion. You can say, "Lord, I want You to help me make something beautiful out of this pain. I had to go through it. It was ugly stuff, but I want it to become a ministry to other hurting people. I know how they feel. I am able to enter into their suffering. God of all compassion, instead of this turning into self-pity and hardness, turn it into compassion." The quickest way out of your pit is to help somebody else out of theirs.

Christ alone can redeem life's big hurts. Why not let Him use it to shape you into a make-a-difference person for other people? Haven't you replayed those ugly scenes enough times? Do you really need to go over it again? Why don't you let Him turn self-focus into others-focus? Look around you. Find a need and meet it. Instead of looking in the mirror at your scars, why don't you surrender yourself to the emotional rebuilding of the master Surgeon? Let Him start changing you from someone who feels like a victim to someone who is beginning to be a victor. Doctor Jesus makes scars into something beautiful.

was flying into a city early one Saturday morning, and as I got off, I saw a TV crew. I thought, "Hmm, somebody important must be on this plane." I looked around and suddenly a microphone was in my face. Obviously, it had nothing to do with somebody important or they wouldn't be talking to me. Well, this happened to be the day after the World Trade Center had been bombed in New York City. I live in the New York area and I was a passenger on a flight from New York the morning after, so they wanted a comment for the evening news. The man who was picking me up told them I was a speaker coming to town, so I would be a good one to interview. So they stuck this microphone in my face and asked, "How does this explosion right in the heart of New York City make New Yorkers feel?" Since I have been many times in the parking lot where the bomb went off, I gave them the first word that came to my mind—vulnerable. We suddenly feel vulnerable. That's how a lot of people feel these days, because a lot of things we have counted on are blowing up. Let's take a God-moment about . . .

A Tower
They Can't Blow Up

Our word from the Word of God comes from Proverbs 18:10. "The name of the LORD is a strong tower; the righteous run to it and are safe." Maybe you are one of those people who says, "Well, I am going to get with the Lord someday . . . I really need to settle things with Him someday." This verse says run to the Lord. You don't wait, you don't postpone, you run to that strong tower when you have the opportunity. The more unstable things become, the more urgent it seems to get into a right relationship with God. We need to depend on a tower that can't be blown up, that can't suffer from a recession, depression, the stock market, a layoff, a takeover, or an illness.

Many of us feel vulnerable these days because of what has been happening to the towers that have always been there for us. You cannot be sure if your company, your job, or your retirement is going to be there. Are your property values going to be there? Is your medical care going to be there? Is your partner going to be there? Is your family going to be there? Maybe you've been in a relationship that once looked like a tower for you, and now that's gone. Frankly, this is no time to be running your own life or depending on some earth stuff or earth tower for security. This is run-to-the-Lord time.

I have handed out four 3 x 5 cards to young people and asked them to write the four most important things in their life on those cards. Then I tell them, "Drop one of those. There's some tragedy and you lose one of those most important things in your life. Which will it be?" They painfully throw a card to the ground. When they are down to three, I ask them to drop one more. Finally, when they're down to two, they look at me like, "I cannot drop either of these," but I say, "You can keep one." With great reluctance, they drop the second most important thing in their life to the ground. I say, "Now, you have that one card with the most important thing in your life. Let me ask you a question about it. Is it something you might unexpectedly lose?"

I would ask you the same question. Maybe this is the day you finally face what God has been trying to tell you—that you are away from Him. Isaiah 59:2 says, "Your iniquities [the running of your own life] have separated you from your God." But Romans 10:13 says, "Everyone who calls on the name of the Lord will be saved." The name of the Lord is a strong tower. When Jesus was named, the angel told Mary and Joseph, "You are to give him the name Jesus, because he will save his people from their sins" (Matt. 1:21). That's what you need. Someone to save you from the wall between you and God, to get you to Him in these unstable times. Surrender your life to Jesus, and the indestructible tower of God is open to you, day or night.

Our kids used to go to sleep singing a little chorus, "Safe Am I in the Hollow of His Hands." In a world where towers are going down right and left, that's a wonderful way to go to sleep at night, knowing you are safe because nothing can touch the tower you are in.

Some of our fun family memories are the times I would read stories to my kids. One of their favorites was *Winnie-the-Pooh,* so we had Winnie-the-Pooh, Piglet, Christopher Robin, and of course, Eeyore, the donkey who usually managed to see the dark side of everything. There always seemed to be something wrong in Eeyore's world. We probably all know two-legged Eeyores. They are people who respond to the pressures and problems of life by throwing a pity party for themselves. The last time I looked in the dictionary, there were 192 words that began with *self-,* but few of them are as damaging as *self-pity.* "Look at poor me. Poor me," says Eeyore. Let's take a God-moment about . . .

The Eeyore Complex

Our word from the Word of God is Nehemiah 8:10. Here is the cure. Nehemiah, who had been through all kinds of burdens, challenges, and attacks, says, "Do not grieve, for the joy of the LORD is your strength." This joy of the Lord has nothing to do with our environment. It has to do with our *invironment.* This joy gives us the ability to look for God in any situation and to ask, "How could God use this? I don't particularly like what is going on right now, but God has okayed it. It had to get through my Father's hands before it could get to me, so where is God at work here?" Focus on what is good about the situation. Or on what *could* be good. Concentrate on the positive.

Sometimes when I am tired and stressed, I hear some Eeyore coming out of my mouth. I start to complain and see the negatives and problems. "This could go wrong. This is bad. Looks pretty bleak." What happens? I make a gray day darker because I drag everybody else down with me with my Eeyore complex. It is amazing how a negative person can be a cloud that blots out the sun for everyone else.

Play back the tape of some of your recent conversations. Do you hear the joy of the Lord, or do you hear "poor me" talk?

I remember a day when I woke up very, very depleted. I had a marathon schedule ahead of me, so I decided in my first conscious moments to focus on Jesus' strength. Sure, I could think about my sore throat and that I only had three hours of sleep, but instead of the negatives, I said, "Today, I'm going to think about the strength of Jesus." Well, I found myself energized for that whole long day by focusing on the joy of the Lord.

Conversely, nothing will de-energize you as fast as complaining, self-pity, and down talk. When you look out a dirty window, everything looks dirty. The joy of the Lord can clean that window. Look for the Lord. Look for His goodness in your day today. Talk up the good things, and if you hear the voice of old Eeyore, turn the page.

I'm the early riser in our family, so it's not uncommon for me to be in the bathroom around 6 A.M., the only one awake. Now, I have made a science of being quiet in the morning so I don't wake up my wife or anyone else who might be sleeping. So I was startled one morning when I heard the gentle strains of a song. I had never heard this in the bathroom before. I recognized the song as "It's a Small World after All." Well, here I am in this already dazed condition. I could not figure out where the music was coming from. Was there a radio on? No radio. An alarm? No. Did somebody leave a music box in here? No music box. I searched high and low. Finally, I found out where it was coming from. Believe it or not, the song was coming from the roll of toilet tissue. Uh-huh. Yes, my wife had rigged the tissue with this little device that plays a song every time you roll that thing. You chuckle and say, "Oh, no!" Well, that's nothing. Downstairs in the main bathroom, it plays "The Star Spangled Banner"! That unexpected music sure got my attention, and it brightened up a bleary time of day. Let's take a God-moment about . . .

Music When You Least Expect It

Our word from the Word of God comes from Acts 16:22–25. Paul and Silas have been preaching the Gospel in Philippi and the crowd is attacking them. It's not a good day. "The crowd joined in the attack against Paul and Silas, and the magistrates ordered them to be stripped and beaten. After they had been severely flogged, they were thrown into prison, and the jailer was commanded to guard them carefully. Upon receiving such orders, he put them in the inner cell and fastened their feet in the stocks. About midnight, Paul and Silas were praying and singing hymns to God, and the other prisoners were listening to them."

Well, God sends a violent and dramatic earthquake that lets Paul and the other prisoners loose, and it ultimately leads to the jailer and his family turning to Christ. But let's go back to the part about Paul and Silas singing at midnight. You say, "Wait, something's wrong with this picture. They have been stripped, flogged, imprisoned, put in stocks, and now they're singing. What's going on here?" You might expect this verse to read, "Paul and Silas were complaining at midnight," or griping or feeling sorry for themselves. Something is not *wrong* with this picture. Something is *right*. This music couldn't have come from anything around them—it had to come from inside them. And it got people's attention. It says the other prisoners were listening. You bet they were! Here are people facing the same hardships you are, except they're doing it with joy rather than a negative attitude.

Maybe you're going through one of life's long nights right now, and you've taken a beating. Maybe you've been stripped of things you care about, or you're in one of those prisons that

---

A positive attitude and joy are not feelings, they are choices.

---

doesn't have walls. How are you handling it? Are you like all the other prisoners, or is Christ inside of you giving you the grace to sing when you would otherwise sink? A positive attitude and joy are not feelings, they are choices. Focus on your Lord, as Paul and Silas did with these hymns. Fill up on Christian music. Quote the verses and the promises. And focus on your opportunity. Paul and Silas probably looked around and said, "Hey, we have a captive audience. There are people watching us now who will see how we respond to this." See, people watch you when you're in the midnight darkness more than any other time. The greatest impact of your life comes at the time of greatest pain. If you let God take this moment, He will give you unexplainable grace and joy that will lift you and everyone around you. No one can ignore your life if it produces music when they least expect it.

always enjoyed the TV show *Mission Impossible.* It always had the same formula. The head of the Mission Impossible force would get a tape with the mission orders on it. The assignment was always something totally impossible. He would pick his crew, and then go for it. And you always knew how it would ultimately end because they never failed. The Mission Impossible Force would always get the job done. Well, I've always wanted to find out how to do the "mission impossible." Let's take a God-moment about . . .

The Mission Impossible Prayer

Our word from the Word of God comes from Nehemiah 1:3–4. While working for the king of Persia, Nehemiah receives word that Jerusalem has been torn down. The walls and gates are in ruins. Nehemiah says, "They said to me, 'Those who survived the exile and are back in the province are in great trouble and disgrace. The wall of Jerusalem is broken down, and its gates have been burned with fire.' When I heard these things, I sat down and wept. For some days I mourned and fasted and prayed before the God of heaven."

Nehemiah faced a mission impossible. He had no idea how that city could ever be rebuilt or that he could even make a difference. Maybe you have a mission impossible right now. Maybe it's medical or financial; a relationship with a friend, spouse, or one of your children; emotional or stress-related; or a mountain that simply will not move. Well, Nehemiah prayed a mission impossible prayer. His prayer in Nehemiah 1 changed the course of history, because that Jerusalem wall was rebuilt in fifty-two days under Nehemiah's leadership. How do we get a happy ending to our mission impossible? By praying like Nehemiah. Five ingredients make up Nehemiah's powerful prayer: intensity, availability, purity, authority, and responsibility.

Intensity. Nehemiah says, "O LORD, God of heaven, the great and awesome God, who keeps his covenant of love with those who love him and obey his commands" (v. 5). There is a big difference between a "Dear God" and an "O Lord" prayer. "Dear God" is the kind we usually pray—the casual "Lord, bless me, help my life, forgive my sins, and bless the missionaries." "O Lord" praying is desperate, urgent, on your face, "Lord, I am powerless in this situation." It is time we did some "O Lord" praying. That's intensity.

Availability. In verse 6, Nehemiah says, "Let your ear be attentive and your eyes open to hear the prayer your servant is praying before you day and night." By praying day and night Nehemiah is saying, "Lord, I'm available. I'm Your servant. I'm a blank piece of paper. I will do anything You ask." We need to come to the Lord with willingness and total availability.

Purity. In verses 6 and 7, Nehemiah confesses "the sins we Israelites, including myself and my father's house, have committed against you. We have acted very wickedly toward you. We have not obeyed the commands." He faced the sin that might have been keeping God from blessing them. The problem here was not the walls or the city being down, but the Israelites' own sin. And we also have to look at that first.

Authority. Nehemiah quotes a promise from the Lord that if God's people would call on Him and turn back to His commands, He would bring His exiled people back (see vv. 8–9). He prays on the authority of the promises of God. We need to quote God's promises to Him and say, "Lord, I come to you on the strength of Your promise." There is authority in that kind of praying.

Responsibility. In verse 11 Nehemiah says, "Give your servant success today by granting him favor in the presence of this man." Then he goes to the king to talk to him about the problem. That is responsibility. We must take a step of faith in God's direction, even though we're unsure of the final outcome.

Have a mission impossible? Well, God gives us answers in Nehemiah's prayer. Go to God's throne room and pray a mission impossible prayer.

Karen and I know all about the creeping disease called "senioritis." We have seen it for years in other teenagers, and then in our own home. It begins with "Okay, I'm a senior now. I don't care about high school anymore." At best, a kid afflicted with senioritis just slacks off until graduation. At worst, he or she becomes irresponsible and even destructive. Of course, some people have the disease for all four years of high school, but usually it afflicts them upon entering their senior year. Senioritis does not bring out the best in anybody at any age. Let's take a God-moment about . . .

The Senioritis Vaccine

Our word from the Word of God comes from Jeremiah 29. The Jews are no longer in Judah. They have been carried away into captivity, and are now in Babylon. They are in a situation where it would be easy for them to have spiritual senioritis because they know that God has them in Babylon for their disobedience and will one day return them to their native country. So they are kind of between living in Babylon and returning to Israel. They could be saying, "Who cares about Babylon? Put it on cruise control. We're going home in a little while. What we do here doesn't matter." But here is God's advice for them in Jeremiah 29:5–8. "Build houses and settle down; plant gardens and eat what they produce. Marry and have sons and daughters; find wives for your sons and give your daughters in marriage, so that they too may have sons and daughters. Increase in number there; do not decrease. Also, seek the peace and prosperity of the city to which I have carried you into exile. Pray to the LORD for it, because if it prospers, you too will prosper."

God is saying, "Make something of this time. Don't have senioritis and act like it doesn't matter." It is like old Caleb in the Book of Joshua, eighty-five years old and not ready to quit, saying, "Lord, give me this mountain to conquer."

Maybe you are at an age or in a situation where you're tempted to put your life on cruise. Maybe you are waiting for the next stage—or just waiting for heaven. Don't sit there and say, "I don't care much about where I am." God is saying, "Bloom where you're planted. Make it count."

I once met a dear eighty-year-old woman whose husband had died. She said, "Ron, I was married to the same man for sixty years. He took such great care of me. It would be so easy

God is saying, "Make something of this time. Don't have senioritis and act like it doesn't matter."

for me to be bitter, and I could be desperately lonely." But she said, "This week, as I've listened to you at this conference, I've decided I'm going to reach out on my own."

She continued, "I'm in a condo filled with lonely people. I'm going to go back there and start writing notes to those people and baking for them and visiting them and sharing God's love with them. I'm going to start giving my life away."

I said, "Well, the Bible says that's the way you find it."

And she said, "Well, I figure that my mother died at eighty-eight, so I have at least eight years to make a difference."

Wow! Even at eighty she's going to find her life by giving it away. That is the vaccine for senioritis and for not caring. Get a mission. That is the best way to find your life. Wherever you are, look for a mission. Don't slow down. Don't hold back. Capture the corner you're in for Christ. When you're living for Jesus, you won't want to waste a day.

Our family has had the privilege to spend some unforgettable ministry days on the Navajo reservation in New Mexico and Arizona. When you are there, you do a lot of driving because that one reservation is the size of West Virginia. Now, the vehicle of choice there is not a car. No, you want a truck. See, many places are only accessible by roads that are steep, bumpy, and full of craters. Driving is a major challenge to the durability of any vehicle—or passenger. So you'll hear many radio advertisements using this one phrase to promote the quality of their truck. This macho voice says, "It's reservation tested." Well, let's take a God-moment about being . . .

Reservation Tested

Our word from the Word of God comes from Luke 4, beginning at verse 1. This is the familiar story of the temptation of Jesus. It says, "Jesus, full of the Holy Spirit, returned from the Jordan." Remember, that is where He had been baptized, the Spirit had come down from heaven in the form of a dove, and He had heard the Father's voice saying, "You are my Son, whom I love; with you I am well pleased" (3:22). For Jesus, this is probably the ultimate spiritual high. Luke continues, "[Then he] was led by the Spirit in the desert, where for forty days he was tempted by the devil. He ate nothing during those days, and at the end of them he was hungry. The devil said to him, 'If you are the Son of God, tell this stone to become bread.' Jesus answered, 'It is written, "Man does not live on bread alone"'" (4:1–4). There are two more temptations that come right at Jesus, and He answers each time with the Word of God. When the devil finally gives up and leaves, it says in verse 14, "Jesus returned to Galilee in the power of the Spirit, and news about him spread through the whole countryside. He taught in their synagogues, and everyone praised him" (vv. 14–15). That was the beginning of the public ministry of Jesus Christ.

A cycle in this incident from Jesus' life repeats many times in your life and mine, or at least in the life of any man or woman God wants to use. First is the Spirit's touch. For Jesus, this came at the baptism at the Jordan River. For us, it happens when the Lord comes in an evident, almost tangible way. Do you remember an experience like that, a season of your life where the Lord was so dramatic in the way He revealed Himself and spoke to you? There was no doubt He was there. No doubt that you had heard from heaven. Well, the Spirit's touch is the first step in the cycle. At the end of the cycle comes the Spirit's triumph. At the end of the story from Luke, Jesus' life exploded into ministry. That cycle ultimately ends in our lives becoming powerful and affecting many other lives.

Did you notice what comes between the Spirit's touch and the Spirit's triumph? The Spirit's test. That is our time to be reservation tested. It's hot, it's bumpy, it's lonely, and we're taking a beating. You ask, "Can we skip that part?" No. Jesus didn't and neither can you or I. There is no dove there. There's no voice from heaven. The devil feels more real than God does, and there's doubt, temptation, and deprivation. Our feelings are not inspired anymore, they're just numb.

Does that sound familiar? You're really still on the road to power, but you have to go through the desert. The Lord said that He put the Old Testament saints in the desert to test what was in their hearts. It's not the spiritual high that makes the work of God in your life real. It's the time when there is no feeling and no outward evidence of God at work. The wilderness isn't the

---

You're really still on the road to power, but you have to go through the desert. It's all part of God's loving plan to make you into a strong player for Him.

---

devil's idea. It's his *opportunity,* but it's the *Spirit's* idea. It's all part of God's loving plan to make you into a strong player for Him. The wilderness proves the reality of what God said to you in the high time. Your Lord leads you into this wilderness to wean you from depending on evidence of Him to depending on Him only. He wants you to test the power of God's Word by facing down the Prince of Darkness with only God's Word in your hand.

You feel more powerful after the Spirit's touch, but really you are more powerful after the Spirit's test. Remember, the reason God is driving you over difficult roads is to make you a powerful vehicle for Him.

The meteor shower was all over the news. It was one of the few times astronomers made the front page. A meteor shower occurs maybe every 130 years when the earth moves into the dust trail of a comet. Since I probably will not be here the next time, I went out at the prescribed time with my trusty binoculars, and my son brought his telescope. We found a place where we could get away from as many lights as possible. Apparently, a lot of other people read the same stuff. Here they were already in various chiropractic poses, trying to see this spectacular meteor shower. Later, they said on the news that there were some meteor fireworks that night. Well, we didn't see any. Just about showtime, the clouds decided to roll in. Let's take a God-moment about . . .

Clouds Blocking the Fireworks

Our word from the Word of God comes from Joshua 7. After the incredible victory at Jericho, the Jews had lost a smaller, less challenging battle at a city called Ai. They had been told not to take any plunder from Jericho or God would judge them. Now, they have lost at Ai. Joshua cannot figure out why. Scripture says, "Then Joshua tore his clothes and fell facedown to the ground before the ark of the LORD, remaining there till evening. The elders of Israel did the same, and sprinkled dust on their heads" (v. 6). These guys are desperate. "What's happening Lord? What went wrong?" Joshua said, "Ah, Sovereign LORD, why did you ever bring this people across the Jordan to deliver us into the hands of the Amorites to destroy us? If only we had been content to stay on the other side of the Jordan!" (v. 7). Joshua, you don't know what the problem really is. The Lord said to Joshua, "Stand up! What are you doing down on your face? Israel has sinned" (v. 8). God's people had been experiencing God's power, victory, and the obvious closeness of the Lord, but something was wrong. Now, Joshua was trying to think of everything—maybe it's this, maybe it's that. He was complaining, "Why can't we see Your brightness anymore, Lord?" It seems to me a little like that night we looked for the meteor fireworks. They were there, but something came between us, keeping us from experiencing them. God says, "Joshua, get up. You are going down the wrong trail here. Israel has sinned." Same Joshua, same Jehovah as Jericho, but God's blessing has been withheld because there is hidden sin. Later in the chapter, after it is dealt with aggressively, the blessing of God returns.

Maybe you have that feeling right now. Something is wrong. Maybe it just isn't like it used to be between God and you. Maybe you are not seeing the power, the victory, and the supernatural things you were seeing, and like Joshua, you're wondering where the blame goes. While you're trying to reason it out, God says, "Sin." Clouds have come between you and a clear look at your Lord. Think about it. Have you dealt with the thing that might be causing God to withhold His blessing? Have you even asked about it? Maybe it's a broken relationship, a resentment that has crept in, the return of an old habit, or a way of thinking. Maybe it's a compromise. Maybe you have returned to self-managing things you had surrendered. Maybe you have been shoving your mate or your family aside or compromising your integrity. The Lord is saying, "That's the reason. That is where the clouds are. That's why you can't see Me." It is the last place we like to look for an answer to what is wrong, but could it be that sin has crept into your camp? Could it be that the clouds of compromise have come between you and the Lord, who once blazed so dramatically through your life?

The Lord Jesus is still producing spiritual fireworks. What He has done before, He wants to do again, but those fireworks can only be seen by those who don't let sin block the view.

You probably have a picture of yourself that you do not like, either on your driver's license, an ID card, or a passport. Now, there is probably a picture of you that you *do* like. That picture is the one that shows your good side, your hair is just right, there is good lighting, and you're smiling. Once, at a conference, there was a lady who really appreciated the ministry of one of my fellow speakers. She asked, "Would you mind if I give you a picture of myself?" He said that would be fine. She signed it and put it in a note, and he didn't look at it until he got to lunch. He opened it and said, "Look at this picture." It was the most unusual personal photo I have ever seen. It was a picture of her hands. Let's take a God-moment about how . . .

The Hands Tell It All

Our word from the Word of God comes from Isaiah 49, beginning at verse 15. God asks the provocative question, "Can a mother forget the baby at her breast and have no compassion on the child she has borne?" The answer, of course, should be never, but it does happen. "Though she may forget," God says, "I will not forget you!" He says, "See, I have engraved you on the palms of my hands." That lady gave my friend a picture of worn, wrinkled hands. You could see that those hands had obviously worked hard for a long time. That is how she wanted to portray her life. Likewise, God seems to be saying here, "If you want to know how I feel about you, look at this picture of Me. Look at My hands."

Do you know what the message is in His hands? "I will never forget you." Look at the hands of God in a stable, in a little town called Bethlehem, where all the power of the Creator is packed into a little Jewish baby. His hands cannot even grab His mother's nose. These are hands that created the world but are now helpless as He becomes a human being.

Look at those hands touching people with healing at the point of their need. Then see those hands nailed viciously to a cross. A few days later, those hands are extended to Thomas to prove that He is alive. Jesus is alive and glorified, but the nail scars are still there. They are our engraving on the palms of His hands.

Maybe you're in a time when other hands have left you or let you down. Maybe the hand you once held isn't there anymore. The hands that paid you or met your material needs may

---

Today, almighty God has His hands open, and He cannot forget you.

---

be closed to you now. The hands that once applauded you may be silent. Even the hands that would like to help you now cannot reach far enough to touch where you're really hurting.

Today, almighty God has His hands open, and He cannot forget you. Nailprints are there because of how much He loves you. And no matter how alone you feel right now, He is offering all the grace, all the love, all the understanding, and all the power you need. God has you deep in His heart, and He is touching you even now. He wants you to know that. You are always on His mind. You are safely in His nail-engraved hands. I cannot help but think of those beautiful hymn words, "I shall know Him when redeemed by His side I shall stand. I shall know my Redeemer when I reach the other side by the print of the nail in His hands."

In college, some of my friends took a missionary aviation course. Missionary pilots are some of my heroes. They fly around the world and land in places you would think a plane could never land. They know how to take their plane apart and put it back together again. They are incredible pilots.

The missionary aviation training course is very demanding. My friends studied on campus for two years, and then, if they made the cut, they would go down south to the flight campus at an airport. On a Friday afternoon, they posted those names, and only half the guys who had put in two years of study would qualify to complete the rest of the course. I watched my friends sweat it out that week. For some of them, I think it might have been the longest week of their lives. Finally, the day came and there was the list. You could hear the shouting of some of the guys who had just experienced one of the most exciting moments in their lives. They found out they had made the list. Let's take a God-moment about . . .

Making Hell's List

Our word from the Word of God comes from Acts 19, beginning at verse 13. "Some Jews who went around driving out evil spirits tried to invoke the name of the Lord Jesus over those who were demon-possessed. They would say, 'In the name of Jesus, whom Paul preaches, I command you to come out.' Seven sons of Sceva, a Jewish chief priest, were doing this. One day the evil spirit answered them, 'Jesus I know, and I know about Paul, but who are you?' Then the man who had the evil spirit jumped on them and overpowered them all. He gave them such a beating that they ran out of the house naked and bleeding." This is an enlightening passage because it appears that the forces of darkness have a list of people who are a threat. The demons said, "We know Jesus. We know Paul. Who are you guys? You're not on the list." The sons of Sceva used the right words and tried to do spiritual things, but they were spiritually powerless.

What a worthy goal to have your name known on a list in hell. Have they ever heard of you there? You don't make the list by attending meetings, believing creeds, saying Christian things, or even holding Christian offices. You make the devil's list by making a difference for Christ.

Maybe you have been under fire lately. Maybe you have felt some pressure physically, financially, medically, emotionally, or maybe in your relationships. It's not time to blame everything on the devil, but it is possible you have made his list. Maybe you're starting to take Jesus seriously for the first time in your life. Maybe you're starting to take some risks to move out for Him, finally moving from being a spectator to being a player for Him. Maybe you're daring to speak out about Jesus to lost people. You might be evaluating your priorities and considering leaving your comfort zone to serve the Lord or step up to spiritual leadership. If you are pushing back the darkness, expect to make Satan's list.

A wise old pastor said, "The ferocity of satanic attack upon you increases in direct proportion to your potential usefulness for Jesus Christ." That is true, but you have nothing to fear. For, "the one who is in you is greater than the one who is in the world" (1 John 4:4). If you know that the turbulence may be coming from the devil, you will get your armor on and fight with spiritual weapons. It may be that nothing is really wrong but is actually very right. Your new commitment to Jesus Christ has set off an alarm bell in hell. When the demons check the list of those who are threats they'll either see your name and say, "Who?" Or they will say, "Oh, yes, we know him or her." When you are making a difference for Jesus Christ, you are on the devil's list. I hope you're on it. Making that list is hell's highest compliment.

M y wife, Karen, is not the typical American TV viewer. First of all, she seldom watches it; and second, when she does, I often find her watching nature shows. Last time I walked in, she was watching a program on whales. It was about how the killer whale is really not as vicious as we might think. They actually had film footage of one floating in the water while smaller animals were playing on him. The commentator said killer whales are usually pretty gentle—and they can afford to be. They know no one can threaten them, because there is no one stronger. Let's take a God-moment about . . .

Never Playing Defense

Our word from the Word of God comes from 1 Peter 2:21–23. "To this you were called, because Christ suffered for you, leaving you an example, that you should follow in his steps." We all know Christ is an example, but if we were to be like Him, what would we do? "'He committed no sin, and no deceit was found in his mouth.' When they hurled their insults at him, he did not retaliate; when he suffered, he made no threats. Instead, he entrusted himself to him who judges justly." Here is Jesus under pressure, under attack, in danger, but He issues no threats, no comebacks, no retaliations, and no angry words. How could He be so undefensive when He is so under attack? Because He could say, "I am in the hands of Someone whose hands are bigger than the hands raised against Me." That brings us back to our killer whales, who are gentle, not because they're weak, but because they know they are strong and secure. No one is bigger.

Maybe sometimes you find yourself under pressure and treated badly. Everything in your human nature says, "Strike back. Give them a taste of their own medicine." But Jesus calls us to follow in His steps, which means no retaliation. Don't strike back, not because you are a weak wimp, but because you are strong in Christ. You don't have to retaliate. You don't have to react. You can be gentle, by your own choice, to those who are harsh, because your Father is strong. Everything important to you is safe in His hands.

The Bible says that one of the fruits of the Spirit is gentleness. Sometimes gentleness is thought of as being weak, but

---

You're in a strong position. If God is for you, who could be against you?

---

gentleness is for the strong in the Lord. Be sure that your agenda, your security, and your concerns have been surrendered fully to your Lord, and then relax. Don't answer back, don't threaten, and don't retaliate. Remember, "A gentle answer turns away wrath" (Prov. 15:1). Your battle is the Lord's. You need to concentrate on playing offense, gaining ground for your Lord. Don't waste time playing defense for yourself. In Christ you are strong, so you can afford to be gentle. You're in a strong position. If God is for you, who could be against you?

They don't make garbage like they used to. Do you remember the good old days when you could throw away everything when you were done with it? Actually, those were not the good old days, because we were also trashing our environment. I don't know how it is in your neighborhood, but once a month we have the privilege of sorting and putting out what used to be just garbage. Bottles, newspapers, cans, and glass are now called recyclables. It is amazing how they can take garbage and then recycle it into something useful again. Let's take a God-moment about . . .

Pieces and Masterpieces

Our word from the Word of God comes from Genesis 50:20. Joseph is speaking to his brothers who left him in a pit and sold him into slavery. Now he is second-in-command of Egypt, saving their lives with the food program he has developed. "You intended to harm me," he said, "but God intended it for good to accomplish what is now being done, the saving of many lives." Joseph had a lot of garbage in his life: broken family relationships, false accusations, imprisonment, and abandonment. Eventually, the great plan of God led him to become assistant pharaoh, giving him, a Jew, authority over Egypt. Then he was able to save thousands of lives, including the lives of his own family, who were the fathers of the twelve tribes of Israel. Up close, this looked like tragedy. When you look at the big picture, it was the tapestry of God.

God is the ultimate recycler. He can take the trash of your life and recycle it into treasure. You have to bring to Jesus what is broken, and He makes pieces into masterpieces. How does He do that? He will do it with His power, if you will do your part in the recycling process.

First, ask the right question. "Why is this happening?" will probably not get an answer. Work on asking, "How could God use this?" Second, tell it all to Jesus. Bring Him all the pieces, all of the darkest feelings you have about what is broken right now. Third, cancel all pity parties. Self-pity will become a prison for you, and the devil wins a victory. Fourth, look for other people who are hurting. Through the hurts of your life, God gives you a brand-new sensitivity. He uses the broken pieces of your life to touch the lives of other people going through the same thing.

You have to bring to Jesus what is broken, and He makes pieces into masterpieces. He uses the broken pieces of your life to touch the lives of other people going through the same thing.

Consider the garbage in your life right now. What is broken? A family? A heart? A budget? A marriage? A child? A body? A dream? Bring Jesus the pieces. Remember, He makes those pieces into masterpieces.

My flight was scheduled to leave Newark at 3:30, but there was bad weather at my destination, so they said we would be delayed until 4:30. Then they said, "We have no idea when we'll be able to leave." And later they said, "We think we'll go at 5:30." Finally, we did leave—at 6:00. Of course, that gave us lots of time to memorize the menu in the little restaurant, check out the restroom several times, buy lots of magazines, and count the designs in the carpet. Well, a canceled flight had joined ours, so this was a very full plane. As passengers lumbered aboard with all their luggage, word came from the cockpit. "Ladies and gentlemen, we are number two for takeoff. We've been assigned that position, but we only have twenty minutes to load this plane and take off, so would you please be seated as quickly as you can, wherever you can." So now we had chaos. People were still boarding the plane, with the captain pushing them verbally and the flight attendants pushing them physically. "Sit anywhere, we have to go. We're going to lose our spot and have to wait longer." First we wait for hours, and then suddenly we're in a mad rush! Let's take a God-moment about . . .

The Miracle Rush

Our word from the Word of God comes from Exodus 12. This is where the Jews are spending their last night as slaves in Egypt. They've been through a long process of waiting while God recruited Moses to be their deliverer and then dealt with Pharaoh. They have been through nine plagues, with things getting worse before getting better. It's the night of Passover. They've applied blood to their doorposts and as the angel passes over, the firstborn sons of Egypt die while theirs are protected. In Exodus 12:11 they get instructions about the Passover dinner. "This is how you are to eat it: with your cloak tucked into your belt, your sandals on your feet and your staff in your hand. Eat it in haste; it is the LORD's Passover." They really did need to be ready quickly because when the Lord moves, it really happens fast. Verses 33–34 say, "The Egyptians urged the people to hurry and leave the country. . . . So the people took their dough before the yeast was added, and carried it on their shoulders in kneading troughs wrapped in clothing." Like the night I had at the airport, they had a long wait followed by a big rush.

Now, there is insight here into what God might be doing in our lives. He works quietly, invisibly, methodically. Meanwhile, we get panicky that we will never take off. But when God has everything ready, we need to fasten our seatbelts! The help will come so quickly, there won't even be time for the bread to rise.

You may think you are running out of time, but God doesn't need much time. God can do in an hour what might take you fifty years, so don't panic just because it's taking longer than you thought. Don't let the wait make you give up or push for your own impatient solution. The flight may be delayed, but it will go when your captain knows everything is ready on your end *and* on the other end. Get ready for the miracle rush when your captain says, "We have immediate clearance. We're taking off."

When I am in a hurry, I don't want to see certain signs on the highway, such as "Reduce Speed" and "Construction Ahead." While on a major road in a metropolitan area once, we had to slow down for a big construction area. They were doing major work, which meant the expressway was going to be slowed down for awhile. My cab driver had a good attitude toward it all. He said, "It's an inconvenience, but it will be so much better when they're done." Let's take a God-moment about how we should . . .

Slow Down
for Construction

Our word from the Word of God comes from Psalm 23, beginning at verse 1. These words have comforted, challenged, and encouraged many people for many years. "The LORD is my shepherd, I shall not be in want. He makes me lie down in green pastures, he leads me beside quiet waters, he restores my soul."

It is a beautiful scene, but there are some potentially troubling words here: He *makes* me lie down. We do slow down rather unwillingly, don't we? God has a lot of ways of putting on the brakes. One visit to the doctor can stop us. Or a child who is in crisis. Or an emergency in the life of someone we love. Maybe God has used bad financial news as the brakes. It could be a dramatic change that we never could have anticipated. The brakes are different, but the result is the same—we get slowed down.

Maybe that is exactly where you are right now. It's possible that you have been traveling at a very high rate of speed. Maybe you have been trying to manage growth, manage a crisis, or build something new. Maybe you have been packing more and more into your life, trying to balance demands from every direction, or trying to make things happen. Suddenly, God has hit the brakes.

Now, you can sit there and mutter and bang on the steering wheel, or you can realize why God is doing this. He knows you need quiet waters right now. You need green pastures. Your soul needs some restoring. You are tired, inside and out. Don't fight it. This is His love in action. He knows you could not keep running at that pace. Maybe you were running over people or past them or neglecting the people closest to you. Maybe you have begun to think that your work is your worth, and He has been crowded to the edge of your life. It's probably time for whatever kind of construction He wants to do.

So if God has slowed you down or shut you down, relax in the knowledge that this is His plan. This is His love. This is His assignment right now, and His way to give you what you need most. Sure, the traffic has braked to a halt. You are in a divine construction zone. God has slowed your speed so He can work on you. But, like that cab driver said, it will be worth the inconvenience. You will be so much better when the construction is finished, so be still and know that He is God.

Our friends were kind enough to loan Karen and me their second home so we could get away for a couple of days. When you are in somebody else's home, you want to be on your good behavior, to make sure you don't break anything, and to leave it as you found it. I was having a little difficulty getting the front door unjammed, or rather, unlocked. Karen asked, "What are you doing?" and I jokingly said, "I couldn't get it unlocked, so I'm just forcing it open." She said, "No! Don't do that!" Now, that was a panicked first reaction, but she had reason to be afraid. I *was* forcing it to open, and I do have a tendency to try to make things work when they don't want to work. I sometimes get impatient with things that don't work quickly. I have been known to force a door handle, a tool, a lock—and break them all. Let's take a God-moment about . . .

When You Force It, You Break It

Our word from the Word of God comes from Genesis 16. Verse 1 says, "Now Sarai, Abram's wife, had borne him no children. But she had an Egyptian maidservant named Hagar; so she said to Abram, 'The LORD has kept me from having children. Go, sleep with my maidservant; perhaps I can build a family through her.'" Verse 4 says, "He slept with Hagar, and she conceived."

Abram and Sarai had been promised a son by God. They had to wait longer than they thought they would have to wait, so guess what Sarai tried to do? "Let's force it. I have an idea . . . we'll help God out." Here is a new verb: "to Hagar." You ask, "Well, isn't Hagar the name of this maidservant and surrogate mother?" Yes, but to me it also means "to try to make it happen." And if you force it, you break it, right?

Fourteen years later, the son God promised them came— Isaac. But now they also have Ishmael on their hands. The mothers of the two boys were in constant conflict, and the boys are still in conflict today—the Arabs and the Jews—and the great wars of the world may be fought over that conflict. All this happened simply because Abram and Sarai couldn't wait for God to do it His way and in His time.

How easy that is to do—force it. Right now, maybe there is something in your life that isn't working as you think it should. Maybe the romance isn't there, and you think you need to help God out a little bit. Maybe the finances aren't there, and you think you need to figure out a way to help God. Maybe the future isn't working out the way you want it to. Maybe a certain person isn't responding, so you are going to push a little bit—and push them away. You're going to break it. Don't *Hagar!* Don't grab a wrong way to get a right thing done. You will pay for that mistake for a long time. Four thousand years later we are still paying for Abram and Sarai's Hagar Solution. Be honest about it. Are you trying to force it right now? Let go before you break it, and let God make it work when He knows it is time.

have been on long airplane flights, but I don't think I have ever been on one that seemed longer than a flight I once had from Newark to Chicago. Normally, it takes about two hours. Leaving on a 3:30 flight for a 7:30 meeting in Chicago is no problem—unless there are thunderstorms for two hours at O'Hare airport, and then the entire air system in America is thrown into total confusion. For starters, we were held over for two and a half hours on the ground before we ever took off in Newark. We said, "Well, that's okay. We'll get to O'Hare a little late, but at least we'll get there." The next thing we knew, the pilot announced we were circling St. Louis, and if you know your geography, you know that St. Louis is not between Newark and Chicago. Then he said we don't have to hold there anymore; we get to hold over southern Illinois instead, so we were in another hold for awhile. Then he said, "Now we can move in closer to O'Hare, but we're running out of fuel." So we were diverted to Milwaukee. I thought, "Well, I'll use one of these in-flight phones to call and make arrangements to get to Chicago." The phones weren't working.

Eventually, we took a bus to Chicago. I got to bed at 3:00 A.M. for the 5:30 session I had later that morning. I remember when we got off the plane, the airline representative said, "Folks, don't blame us. This was just an act of God." Well, that's usually a legal term, but maybe it's more than that. Let's take a God-moment about . . .

Accident or Assignment?

Our word from the Word of God comes from the Old Testament book of Nahum. This is probably not a book of the Bible you were talking about at the breakfast table this morning. But Nahum 1:3 is a great verse. "His way is in the whirlwind and the storm." When a storm is going on, everything is out of control and everybody's plans change. My plans sure changed that one flight day, but usually that happens when many acts of God happen. See, I had a lot of time on the plane to share in-depth about Christ with Scott, a young dad who sat next to me. Then, on that bus from Milwaukee to Chicago, God placed me near a young gal who has been involved in a cult from the time she was a little girl, and we were able to speak of Christ for the entire trip. I believe God had this in mind all the time. Even when things appear out of control, they are under control. His control.

Even when things appear out of control, they are under control. His control.

Remember, this is the day the *Lord* has made, not the weather, your boss, your kids, the doctor, or the bank. David shares a great perspective on life in Psalm 16:5–6. He says, "LORD, you have assigned me my portion and my cup; you have made my lot secure. The boundary lines have fallen for me in pleasant places; surely I have a delightful inheritance." That is the psalm of a settled person. Whatever comes into my life today is not an accident—it is a divine assignment. When you call Jesus "Lord," He has the right to assign you to that situation today or for many days. He will send you the assignment that will bring glory to Christ and put you right in the middle of God's work on earth, whether it feels like it to you or not. Now, He might assign you a big job or a little job, a big group or a little group, a hospital bed or a spotlight, a job or an unemployment line, America or another part of the world, a traffic jam or a circling airplane. Any assignment given by the God who loves you is the best possible place you can be, and that is where you are right now.

Your day is really an act of God. Instead of griping over a situation, look for the Lord in it. He is having His way in the storm, so celebrate wherever you are today. You have been trusted by God with an assignment from Him.

Many of the world's greatest dramas are not on a stage or a screen. They are played out in that quadrennial spectacle we call the Olympics. One year Britain's representative in the 400-meter race, Derek Redmond, went down in the back stretch with a torn right hamstring. As the medical attendants approached, Redmond fought to his feet and set out hopping, desperately trying to finish the race. He knew he wouldn't win, he was just trying to finish. When he reached the final stretch, a large man in a T-shirt came out of the stands, pushed a security guard out of the way, ran to Redmond, and hugged him. That big man was Jim Redmond, Derek's father, and he said to him, "Son, you don't have to do this." Gritting his teeth and with tears in his eyes, his son said, "Yes, I do." His father said, "Well, then, we're going to finish this together." They fought off the security men who were trying to pull Dad off the track, and Derek's head was sometimes buried in his father's shoulder, but they stayed in his lane to the end. When they crossed the finish line, the crowd, stunned at first, stood to its feet. The crowd howled and wept as those two men finished the race. Let's take a God-moment about . . .

Father to the Finish

Our word from the Word of God comes from Deuteronomy 1, beginning at verse 29. Moses says to Israel, "Then I said to you, 'Do not be terrified; do not be afraid of them. The LORD your God, who is going before you, will fight for you, as he did for you in Egypt, before your very eyes, and in the desert. There you saw how the LORD your God carried you, as a father carries his son, all the way you went until you reached this place.'" Maybe today you are tired, banged up, or stressed out, and like that 400-meter runner in the Olympics, you are staggering right now. You're having a hard time finishing your race. You started well, and you have been running hard, but you're about to go down. Maybe you have been hit by discouragement, illness, family trouble, a lack of support, or a lack of help. Maybe you've run into obstacles or pain, and you are hurting, and there is still more of the race ahead of you. Well, God wants to give you the good news that someone has left the stands to help you. He is coming to the track to get you the rest of the way. It's your Father, your heavenly Father.

Well, God wants to give you the good news that someone has left the stands to help you. He is coming to the track to get you the rest of the way. It's your Father, your heavenly Father.

First, God left the stands to come to the cross, and there He rescued us from the sin wounds that would have kept us from ever reaching heaven. He knows we can't make it alone. He is an all-powerful Father who offers to carry us, but we have to let Him. If we are too proud to collapse in His arms and surrender to His control, then our power is limited, and we're not going to make it. If we will totally release the control and, in the words of Scripture, humble ourselves, we will have all His power. Even little children know where the power is when they sing, "They are weak, but He is strong. Yes, Jesus loves me."

Each of us reaches days when we just don't have any more to give. Maybe you're there now. It's *those* moments in the race that can take you deeper into the love and power of Jesus than you have ever been before. Your Father is not a spectator in the stands today. His arm is around you right now, where you are. Listen to His voice saying, "We're going to finish this . . . together!"

Did you ever try a soap sandwich? If so, it was probably when you were little, when you said some words you weren't supposed to say. It seems logical that your parents would want to clean out your mouth after saying words like that, right? Well, that is a punishment that does motivate you to not want to say that particular thing again. But there are some words far dirtier than the words we ate soap for. They are dirty because they deeply hurt many people. Prepare yourself for some dirty words. Let's take a God-moment about . . .

What to Do with Life's Dirty Words

Our word from the Word of God is from Romans 8, beginning at verse 35 and ending with my life verse in verse 37. "Who shall separate us from the love of Christ? Shall trouble or hardship or persecution or famine or nakedness or danger or sword?" It's a pretty dark list, isn't it? Verse 36 continues, "As it is written: 'For your sake we face death all day long; we are considered as sheep to be slaughtered.' No, in all these things we are more than conquerors through him who loved us." This is an amazing passage. Paul gives a laundry list of the worst things life can throw at us, but he says we'll come out winners.

Here are some dirty words. Cancer. You hear the doctor say it to someone you love. That is one of life's dirty words. Divorce. Fired. Bankrupt. Alone. Death. Maybe you'd want to add other dirty words. They are dirty because of the way they hurt us or someone we love. They comprise our greatest fears. They are icebergs that can sink even the most Titanic people, but Paul says Jesus makes the difference. He says, "Through Christ, through Him, I can be more than a conqueror."

The test of the worth of what you are living for is this: Does it hold you together when everything collapses? How can you handle these dirty words of life? You say, "I'm not sure I could." Well, you can because God increases His grace as the demands increase. He gives cancer-grace for cancer, divorce-grace for dealing with a broken family, and bankruptcy-grace for financial problems. I have seen it. I have seen it in Linda as she stood by her husband's casket where she comforted *me,* saying, "Jesus is enough." I saw it as Jim and Terry faced their five-year-old daughter's death from leukemia. I saw it as Mark lost his business almost overnight. I have experienced that conquering love at my wife's bedside when she almost died from hepatitis.

Paul says in Romans 8:32, "He who did not spare his own Son, but gave him up for us all—how will he not also, along with him, graciously give us all things?" He met your greatest need at the cross. What need can He *not* meet? This is an inseparable relationship. When you face one of life's dirty words, you can answer back, "You can't touch Jesus. You can't touch my relationship with Him."

I remember the year my favorite football team, the New York Giants, won only three games in their entire season of sixteen games. That was also the year an airplane flew over Giants' stadium with a little banner attached that said, "Fifteen years of lousy football is enough." That was the year people had little meetings in the parking lot and burned their season tickets. But I rooted for the Giants even then. I also remember going crazy when the Giants won the Super Bowl. As their losses started to become victories over the years, it was amazing how many fans the Giants suddenly picked up. What those fans don't know and will never know is that the best celebration is for those who were there when everybody else was abandoning the team. *We* really won. Let's take a God-moment about being . . .

Loyal
in the Losing Seasons

Our word from the Word of God comes from John 20:1. What great news! "Early on the first day of the week, while it was still dark, Mary Magdalene went to the tomb and saw that the stone had been removed from the entrance." What is this all about? This is the first Easter. Verse 11 continues, "But Mary stood outside the tomb crying. As she wept, she bent over to look into the tomb and saw two angels in white, seated where Jesus' body had been, one at the head and the other at the foot. They asked her, 'Woman, why are you crying?' 'They have taken my Lord away,' she said, 'and I don't know where they have put him.' At this, she turned around and saw Jesus standing there, but she did not realize that it was Jesus. 'Woman,' he said, 'why are you crying? Who is it you are looking for?' Thinking he was the gardener, she said, 'Sir, if you have carried him away, tell me where you have put him, and I will get him.' Jesus said to her, 'Mary.' She turned toward him and cried out in Aramaic, 'Rabboni!' (which means Teacher)" (vv. 11–16).

No one celebrated on Easter morning like Mary Magdalene because she had been there through every winning and losing season. Jesus appears first to the person who was the last to leave Him, and He still does that today. Mary Magdalene is the model of loyal love for Jesus.

Are you a model of that? You say, "I love Him." Well, look at Mary Magdalene. Matthew 27:55 says that she and some of the other women "had followed Jesus from Galilee to care for his needs" (see also Luke 8:2–3). She loved Him enough to leave her security—have you done that? She loved Him enough to sacrifice her money for Him—do you do that? She loved Him enough to stand by Him when it was totally dark—do you? She still did things out of love when her emotional tank was empty. She got spices together for His grave because she loved Him. The test of your love for Jesus isn't how excited you get in the meetings, how many meetings you go to, how many offices you hold, how many verses you know, or what plaques and stickers you have. Are you loyal when there is nothing but darkness? When it looks like it's over? When the feelings are gone?

The loyal fans have the most to celebrate when Jesus wins, and He will win. Jesus comes personally to encourage the one who stands by Him in the darkest of times, and you get to see Him as the fair-weather fans will never see or know Him. Right now, as a loyal fan, Jesus will move in by you and speak your name, and you will be able to say, as only His loyal supporters can, "I have seen the Lord."

THE PEOPLE YOU LOVE

Deepening Your Relationship with Your Family

Let's take a time-out for some exercise. Do this exercise only if both hands are available. Extend one hand so it's out straight. Now, poke your index finger full force into your open palm. Next, instead of poking with your finger, hit that hand full force with your fist. Which one had more power? Let's take a God-moment about . . .

The Power of a Fist

Our word from the Word of God comes from Nehemiah 4, beginning at verse 12. Nehemiah has rallied the Jews to begin rebuilding the wall of Jerusalem, which has been down for many years. The gates have been burned, and all kinds of animals and enemies are getting in and out of there. But now that the wall is going up, people who are opposed to the repairs are threatening to attack. Nehemiah 4:12 says, "Wherever you turn, they will attack us."

Here is how Nehemiah fights back. "Therefore I stationed some of the people behind the lowest points of the wall at the exposed places, posting them by families, with their swords, spears and bows. After I looked things over, I stood up and said to the nobles, the officials and the rest of the people, 'Don't be afraid of them. Remember the Lord, who is great and awesome, and fight for your brothers, your sons and your daughters, your wives and your homes.'" It is interesting to see how Nehemiah organizes people to fight when there is a threat. It says here that he posted them by families. They had been working independently, but he got them all together in family groupings and then says, "I want you to fight, not for the city, I want you to fight for your family, for your brothers and sons and daughters" and so on. He is talking about the power of fighting as a unit when the pressure is on.

This is like the power of independent fingers. Look at your five fingers right now, stretched apart from each other. Then look at the power of those fingers working as one unit in a fist. The devil knows the power of a church that is a fist, so what do you think he focuses his attack on? Dividing God's people. Maybe you can see it in the church you're involved in. Don't fall for it. Don't waste any ammunition on each other. Save it all for the real enemy. The devil knows the power of a family that is pulling together in a crisis, so he wants to use the crisis to get you to turn on each other. A crisis in a family, in a church, or in a ministry can either divide us into fingers working alone or unite us into a fist that has knockout power.

A crisis in a family, in a church, or in a ministry can either divide us into fingers working alone or unite us into a fist that has knockout power. Whatever situation you are in, help people stay together.

Whatever situation you are in, help people stay together. Encourage them to confront their differences. Get people with differences in a room, kneeling together, praying together, and making a covenant with each other to aim all their ammunition at the real enemy—the devil, who is trying to divide us. He knows that a kingdom divided against itself cannot stand. Be the one who makes the people around you make a fist, and use that fist to knock out the enemy.

A boy from the south side of Chicago meets a girl from the Ozarks of Arkansas, and they live happily ever after. That is my life story. That's Karen and me. As we approached our wedding day a week after our college graduation, we had a lot of love. We didn't have any money to match, so we prayed for our own little wedding miracle. We were also heading into full-time Christian ministry, and there was not going to be much income from it. So we prayed that God would lead people in buying gifts for our wedding that would provide what we needed to set up housekeeping. We didn't need a lot, but we couldn't even afford the basics. We prayed that there wouldn't be much duplication in the gifts. Well, there was hardly any. It was amazing. We received one of each of the things we needed, except we got four teakettles. Don't ask me to explain that. You could do a gospel quartet with them.

As we opened the presents, it looked as if God Himself had shopped for our wedding gifts. We got everything we needed because one wedding Guest made all the difference. Let's take a God-moment about . . .

Marriage Miracles

Our word from the Word of God comes from John 2, beginning at verse 1. "On the third day a wedding took place at Cana in Galilee. Jesus' mother was there, and Jesus and his disciples had also been invited to the wedding. When the wine was gone, Jesus' mother said to him, 'They have no more wine.'" Verse 6 continues, "Nearby stood six stone water jars, the kind used by the Jews for ceremonial washing, each holding from twenty to thirty gallons. Jesus said to the servants, 'Fill the jars with water'; so they filled them to the brim. Then he told them, 'Now draw some out and take it to the master of the banquet.'" They probably thought, "I don't think he's interested in water." But "they did so, and the master of the banquet tasted the water that had been turned into wine." Verse 11 says, "This, the first of his miraculous signs, Jesus performed in Cana in Galilee. He thus revealed his glory." Notice what brought Jesus to Cana that day. It was a marriage. Notice where He did His first miracle, at a wedding. We saw our personal miracle at our wedding, and we have seen a lot since.

Well, maybe your marriage could use a miracle right now. That day in Cana there was a change that no man or woman could make. Nobody can change water into wine, but Jesus did. There was a need that no man or woman could ever meet, but Jesus did. Maybe right now, some change is urgently needed in your home. There is a need that must be met if your relationship is going to be what it needs to be. Maybe it is time for Cana revisited—a marriage miracle. Right now there's strain, distance, resentment, and frustration. Maybe there are thoughts of bitterness, and giving up.

Have you been to your knees together yet? Have you prayed—not "Lord, bless the missionaries and bless the world," but poured out your mess, your pain, and your dark feelings to the Lord—crying out together for Jesus' healing in your marriage? The less you feel like doing it, the more you need to. And if your partner absolutely will not, don't let that stop you. This passage says Jesus had been invited to this wedding, to this marriage. Why don't you invite Him into your marriage? Close the door to leaving or quitting. Ask God to show you the hope factors that you can build on. You have looked at the hopeless factors enough. Can you pray this? "Lord, we can't make it work, and I don't know how You would, but we beg You to do what we can't do in this marriage."

Two thousand years ago, in the midst of a marriage, Jesus met an impossible need with His supernatural intervention. Today, the scene is set again with you and the one you have promised your life to. The couple, the need . . . the miracle.

It travels six thousand miles and still hits its target. I have a hard enough time hitting a dartboard halfway across the room. I'm talking about an intercontinental ballistic missile. I saw several when I visited an air force base not long ago. It carries this nuclear payload that has incredible power. The amazing thing is that this missile can get to its target so accurately. It's a good thing that it can. I hope that it will never be launched, but if it is, you sure wouldn't want that missile wandering off course somewhere with all that power. Can you imagine a missile that powerful with no guidance system? Let's take a God-moment about . . .

A Guidance System for the Missiles at Home

There's a sign in our kitchen that my wife put up, and it connects parenting to this mental picture of a missile. It says, "Children are messengers we send to a time we will not see." Sounds like they're going to be our missiles to the future, doesn't it? But so many things can pull them off course. Today, a lot of parents look in the eyes of their son or daughter and wonder, "Man, do I have what they need in a world like this?" Well, challenging parenting is nothing new.

Our word from the Word of God is found in Deuteronomy 6, where all of a sudden parents were having to raise their kids in a pagan culture, filled with pornography, promiscuity, godlessness, and sophisticated temptations. But God tells them to raise their children there. Now, here are His instructions in Deuteronomy 6, beginning at verse 5. "Love the LORD your God with all your heart and with all your soul and with all your strength. These commandments that I give you today are to be upon your hearts. Impress them on your children. Talk about them when you sit at home and when you walk along the road, when you lie down and when you get up." This is God's antidote to the poison of a dangerous world: a contagious love relationship with the Lord. You have this love for Him upon your heart, then that impresses your children, and they end up being stable people who also love the Lord. I'm not talking about religion. This is a deep relationship with God that steers you through each day. A God that's in your life, not just around it. He is an inner guidance system that pulls you His way in each choice and gives you the strength to do it. But it has to start with you having it. It's supposed to be upon your heart.

Now, I think a lot of us have the Lord in our head. We have the facts, we go to the religious meetings, we know the verses, we know the rituals, we know the hymns. If the way to God was a doctrine test, an attendance record, or a vote of the people who know us, we would do fine. But He says, "I have to be in your heart. That's where I have to be."

There's nothing like a child to show you that you have a Savior in your head but not in your heart. Only a living Savior, whom you've invited into the control room of your life, can make you what your son or daughter needs. When you look into the inquiring or hurting eyes of that boy or girl, you realize they are a mirror of you and you can't meet their needs until you know what to do with your own. That's where the word *Savior* comes in. The Bible says we're doomed to repeat our parents' and our grandparents' mistakes unless . . . well, 1 Peter 1:18–19 has help. It says, "For you know that it was

Invite Him into your heart, the center of you. Then you can infect your son or daughter with a contagious love relationship with the Lord.

not with perishable things such as silver or gold that you were redeemed from the empty way of life handed down to you from your forefathers, but with the precious blood of Christ, a lamb without blemish or defect." Christ died to forgive the sin that scars those I love, to break the power of selfishness that poisons our home. If you are parenting, don't go another day without a personal Savior, without Jesus. Invite Him into your heart, the center of you. Then you can infect your son or daughter with a contagious love relationship with the Lord. If the young missiles at your house can catch that guidance system from you, their life will always be on target.

When you drive in the New York area, lane switching becomes an art. Of course, the danger zone is your blind spot. That one area you can't see in any of your mirrors is pretty critical. Actually, the words *blind spot* have taken on new meaning for my wife, Karen, and me. She has had some vision problems lately and developed what the doctor believes to be a temporary blind spot. He injected some dye to see how much of her vision was blocked, and I was surprised as the doctor showed us the results. He said, "Now, here is the blind spot that we all have." I said, "I do?" Right around the optic nerve, there are no rods and cones to produce a visual image, so we all have a blind spot. Let's take a God-moment about . . .

How to See through Your Blind Spot

Our word from the Word of God comes from the great wisdom of the Book of Proverbs. Proverbs 15:12 is practical stuff. "A mocker resents correction; he will not consult the wise." Verse 5 says, "Whoever heeds correction shows prudence." Now, this is mentioned three times in the same chapter, so it must be important. Verse 32 says, "He who ignores discipline despises himself, but whoever heeds correction gains understanding." It is pretty clear what God is saying here. Wise people know how to accept correction and criticism. We need the people around us who confront us, challenge us, and even criticize us. Why? Because we have a blind spot. We all do. We all have weaknesses we cannot see. There are hurtful ways we treat people, ways we say things, ways we act when we're busy or tired, ways we abuse the truth or people's feelings or some biblical boundary. Some of our most entrenched sins are often sins we cannot see very well. We are so used to doing things a certain way that we will never see some sins without the help of someone else.

God doesn't want our blind spot to remain there, because He knows it can make us crash. So He puts mirrors with two legs into our lives. Do you have some two-legged mirrors in your life? Those are people who love us enough, or maybe even dislike us enough, to tell us the hard truth about ourselves. If you are married, are you letting your mate be your mirror? Sometimes a parent is your mirror. Your child, even a young child, can be God's unblinding agent in your life. He may use a friend. Proverbs 27:17 says, "As iron sharpens iron, so one man sharpens another." Maybe He will even use our enemies. There is some measure of truth in their words or they wouldn't have said them. Keep the percentage that is true, and throw out the rest.

If you are going to be a good mirror for other people, be sure that you show them their strong points too. Many times, we are blind to what is good about us as well as what is bad. Make sure there is praise as well as constructive criticism that says, "I love you enough to tell you the truth."

Even if our physical vision is perfect, we do all have blind spots. But because God loves us so much, He is not going to leave us blind. When someone shows you what you cannot see yourself, be wise enough to take a good look, and don't throw something at the mirror.

When I was on a mission in England and Ireland, I had a day to spend in the historic English city of York. What a place! Surrounded by a medieval wall, it is dominated by a cathedral that might be second only to Westminster Abbey in London. There was an unusual scene out in front—an artist on his knees, painstakingly working on a chalk drawing on the sidewalk in front of the cathedral. When I moved closer and took a look at it, I saw it was the Mona Lisa. He must have been working on it all day. It was beautifully done. As I went inside a restaurant, I saw the artist had left. Within minutes, a little boy came up, intentionally ran over the artwork, then stomped back and forth and made footprints all over it. Other kids followed him and did the same thing. They trampled all over an artist's hard work. It hurts to see someone doing that. Let's take a God-moment about . . .

Trampling on a Masterpiece

Our word from the Word of God comes from Ephesians 4:29–30. "Do not let any unwholesome talk come out of your mouths, but only what is helpful for building others up according to their needs, that it may benefit those who listen. And do not grieve the Holy Spirit of God." God is saying don't tear somebody down with your words. Don't trample them with your words. Why does it bother Him so much? Why does it grieve and break the heart of the Holy Spirit of God?

Turn back to Ephesians 2:10. It says, "We are God's workmanship, created in Christ Jesus to do good works, which God prepared in advance for us to do." Every person is God's unique masterpiece of creation. And He has a job for each of us to do. He is trying to build us up and help us know what that job is. In a world that tears down our worth so much, He tries to get us to believe we are His workmanship in Christ Jesus. No matter how difficult a person we may be, or how obscured the work of God might be, He is trying to finish a work of art in the person He created. That is why it hurts Him so much when we trample on one another.

In angry, impatient, or critical moments, have you left some verbal footprints on your son or daughter? The social scientists tell us that our kids need seven positives to come back to zero after they have heard just one negative. We never forget

---

Have you left some verbal footprints on your son or daughter? Every time you fire careless words at your children or husband or wife, you have been ripping a person God is trying to build.

---

the names we are called or things we are accused of by a parent. I'm sure you haven't forgotten. Every time you fire careless words at your children or husband or wife, when you're tired or you want to win or you want to get your way, you have been ripping a person God is trying to build.

What about attacks the other person doesn't even hear? Maybe damaging words have been said at work, at church, among friends, behind their back. You're still trampling on God's work, marking them up in the eyes of others. We don't usually do trampling with our feet, we do it with our mouths. I can still see those footprints on the artist's skillful work in front of the cathedral, and it was ugly. It is just as ugly when you do it to somebody else with your mouth.

Maybe it is time you did something about the footprints you have left on a masterpiece of God. Maybe it's time you go back and make it right, and make a commitment to not ever again let your mouth mark up the artwork of God.

was excited to work on the Billy Graham Crusade at the Meadowlands in New Jersey. It was well organized. One thing that was especially well organized was security. With thousands of people coming and going, security had been very well thought out. I was honored to be the chairman of that crusade, but I was stopped if I didn't have my proper badge. It didn't matter what your title was, if you didn't wear your badge, you couldn't get any farther. One night as we were entering the arena, one of Mr. Graham's staff was with me, and he had forgotten his badge. Well, when the guard stopped us, I had my badge, so I was able to explain to him who this gentleman was, and they knew who I was. I said, "He really is honest and okay, and he really is on Mr. Graham's staff," so he finally got in on my credentials. Well, that worked . . . there. Let's take a God-moment about . . .

Getting In
on Someone Else's Badge

Our word from the Word of God comes from Romans 14. The second half of verse 10 says, "We will all stand before God's judgment seat." Verse 12 says, "So then, each of us will give an account of himself to God." When we are judged by God, we will be one-on-one with Him. Nobody will be standing there with us. Some people hope to make it with God because of their connections, like my friend from the Billy Graham staff who got in on my badge. Well, no one else's badge will count when we stand before God. We might try to say, "Well, Lord, my parents were great Christians, and my wife is a dear spiritual lady. Think about how much my son, my daughter, was really into this, Lord. My brother is in the ministry. My grandmother has prayed for me for years, and she prays all the time. She's really religious." Maybe we could try other connections and say, "Lord, I was a good Presbyterian. I was connected to the Baptists. I was a good Catholic." None of your connections will matter to God. Nobody else's faith will matter to God. Everyone will have to account for themselves to God. We might say, "Well, I spent years in the church." Billy Sunday said years ago, "Being in church will not make you a Christian anymore than being in a garage will make you a car."

In 2 Timothy 1:5 Paul says of Timothy, "I have been reminded of your sincere faith, which first lived in your grandmother Lois and in your mother Eunice and, I am persuaded, now lives in you also." God has no grandchildren. You must have your own relationship with Him. You must have a badge of your own. Have you been to the cross? That's the badge that gets you into heaven. I have been to the cross. I have been there to have my sins forgiven. You have to go for yourself, for *your* sin, exercising *your* faith. No one else can open the door of your heart. Maybe you feel God's knocking right now. Listen to it. Open up. All the other people you know who belong to Christ will not get you into heaven. They just make you all the more responsible because you have had so many chances.

If you are not sure you have a badge of your own, get to the cross today. Don't miss heaven because you thought someone else could get you in.

Our college son was late getting in one night, so Karen and I were playing our usual roles in a late-night crisis. She usually tosses and turns, wondering what might have happened. I usually sleep through it all. Our son had taken an elderly car with a group of friends to a town that was about two hours away. They were on unfamiliar roads, and the weather wasn't that great. It was 2 A.M., long after the time he should be back. I eventually woke up for this one. Finally, in the middle of the night, the door opened, and there stood the son we had been praying for. We hugged him and told him we loved him. We didn't say, "Where's the car?" We said, "We love you." The fact is, the car broke down—it was still two hours away—but he was back safely. Our values are easily clarified at a time like that. If the person is okay, who cares about the vehicle? Let's take a God-moment about . . .

The Irreplaceables

Our word from the Word of God comes from Acts 27. The apostle Paul is being taken by cargo ship to a trial in Rome. Unfortunately, this ship, loaded with grain for the emperor, has encountered a hurricane-force storm that blows it around for days. It looks like everyone will die. Then an angel appears to Paul in the middle of the night, and Paul reports that to the people on the ship. He says, "I urge you to keep up your courage, because not one of you will be lost; only the ship will be destroyed. Last night an angel of the God whose I am and whom I serve stood beside me and said, 'Do not be afraid, Paul. You must stand trial before Caesar; and God has graciously given you the lives of all who sail with you'" (vv. 22–24). Notice that he says, "None of you will be lost, only the ship." This passage could be a great values clarifier for you, especially if you're in a storm right now. The value system here is this: "It's okay if the ship is lost, it's the people that really matter." It's okay if the car is in trouble, it's not okay if my son is. The people are the irreplaceables. It's amazing how a storm changes our values. Imagine saying to the captain before the trip that all the cargo would be thrown overboard. "What do you mean? I have to keep this cargo. It's my livelihood." Well, he did get rid of all the cargo. It turned out that what he thought he had to have, he didn't have to have. The storm clarified that.

Maybe you have accumulated things in your life, and God is trying to say through the storm, "All those commitments, all those activities, all that stuff that you had to have, you don't

---

Save the people. Don't let the storm blow your family apart. Let it blow you together.

---

have to have. That's why I have sent the storm to you. I want you to see that the cargo items that really matter are the people." It is interesting that God says, "Only the ship." It will be hard if your project fails, your business fails, or the organization doesn't make it, but it's okay. Save the *people.* Don't let the storm blow your family apart. Let it blow you together. Don't let the storm make you care less about the people around you, let it make you care more. Don't let the storm make you withdraw, let it make you reach out.

My son's car is important to me, but my son is a lot more important. If he's okay, we'll worry about the vehicle later. Maybe God has given you some uncertain days lately so you will remember what is expendable and what, or who, is irreplaceable. Invest in the irreplaceables.

My wife and I were on a long drive across the U.S. You'd think it would make sense for me to share the wheel with my wife, right? She's a good driver, and we cover a lot of ground when she's at the wheel, but I hate to let her drive. I will hang on to that wheel as long as I can, and she will ask, "Honey, why don't you let me drive?" Frankly, I find riding gets aggravating very quickly. Finally, my eyes are at half-mast, and I am doing all these creative exercises, pinching myself, flexing, and everything I can to try to stay awake. She says, "Honey, don't you think it's time?" Reluctantly, I say, "Okay, you drive." I will not let go until I cannot drive anymore. Men! Let's take a God-moment about . . .

Control Freaks

Our word from the Word of God comes from 2 Kings 5, which tells the story of a military leader named Naaman, who was "commander of the army of the king of Aram. He was a great man in the sight of his master and highly regarded, because through him the LORD had given victory to Aram. He was a valiant soldier, but he had leprosy" (v. 1).

This is one battle Naaman could not win. All of his might, all of his power, and all of his strategy could not conquer his leprosy. So he went to see Elisha, the man of God in Israel, and received instructions to go bathe in the Jordan River. Verse 10 says, "Go, wash yourself seven times in the Jordan, and your flesh will be restored." But he complains and grumbles, "'Are not . . . the rivers of Damascus, better than any of the waters of Israel? Couldn't I wash in them and be cleansed?' So he turned and went off in a rage" (v. 12). Fortunately, he listened to what his servants said and bathed in that river, and he was finally healed.

Naaman was basically saying, "I know I have a problem bigger than I am. I'll go to God, but I will fix it my way, on my terms." That is still one of our greatest problems. That is why we miss the real power of God and say, "I have to drive." We will give God everything. We will give Him money, time, service, loyalty, and belief. We will give God everything, but not control.

Often, especially with men, God has to strip us to teach us how strong He is and to teach us dependency. Maybe He will use a child in your life that you cannot seem to control. Maybe He will use unemployment or an illness or an injury. Perhaps He'll even use a marital breakdown, asking, "Will you let go of the wheel?"

Unfortunately, we don't seem to learn this lesson once and for all. We have to keep learning it. Men live in unnecessary poverty because we try to do everything with God's help but not His control. We are control freaks, and God wants to break that in us so we can know His power.

Are you like me, not letting go of the wheel until you cannot drive anymore? Well, this moment of weakness you are in right now could introduce you to strength you have never imagined. And everyone close to you will be able to tell that you have finally let go of the wheel. What a relief for you. What a relief for them. You will learn to enjoy the trip much more when Jesus is driving.

There is one sure way to collect a crowd at our house. Just walk slowly through the house with a large, flat, white, square box. That means . . . pizza! You will get that Pied Piper feeling. Show me a big white pizza box, and I will be your follower. I will come running. Have you ever noticed that most pizza boxes say the same thing? "You've tried the rest, now try the best." Somebody has to be wrong about that. I'm surprised we ever noticed anything on the box, because the box does not matter. Who spends time admiring the box? We attack that box to get what is inside. Let's take a God-moment about . . .

The Container Hang-Up

Our word from the Word of God comes from 1 Peter 3:3–4. "Your beauty should not come from outward adornment. . . . Instead, it should be that of your inner self, the unfading beauty of a gentle and quiet spirit, which is of great worth in God's sight." God says here that what really matters is the inner self, not outward adornment. Proverbs 31 talks about a woman who is praised by her children, fully trusted by her husband, and admired by all those around. She is the woman everyone wants to be. Proverbs 31:10 says, "A wife of noble character who can find?" What's the secret? Her noble character. Proverbs 31:30 says, "Charm is deceptive, and beauty is fleeting; but a woman who fears the LORD is to be praised."

Now, the secret is her relationship with the Lord. What makes a woman valuable are the contents inside the container. How's that for a radical idea in a world where a woman's worth is usually measured by her figure and her face? Women look at a beautiful model in a fashion magazine, compare themselves, and say, "I don't look like that." Of course, the model has been worked on for hours by the finest hairdressers and makeup artists, she has special lighting, then one photo out of 150 is selected—and they airbrush that one! *She* doesn't even look like that. That woman doesn't exist.

Both men and women have bought the sad lie that the pizza box is what matters instead of the pizza. We cannot stop the world around us from being superficial, but as followers of Jesus we can do better than that. Women who don't feel they measure up physically usually tend to withdraw and become negative and bitter. They give up on themselves and get discouraged. They kill the beauty inside that really matters, because they are so focused on what they feel they don't have on the outside. God's Word teaches us that our body is just an earth suit, a soul carrier. While we cannot choose to be physically beautiful, a person can choose to be beautiful inside. Not every woman can be gorgeous, but any woman can be radiant. The Bible says to go for the inner glow, to be a woman who makes other people feel important, who promotes others rather than herself, and who develops a joyful, daily walk with Jesus Christ. It is time that God's men and women go after the royal radiance that a prince or princess of God can have. That's what makes a woman a friend worth knowing and a partner worth loving for a lifetime.

Don't chase what you want to marry, instead be what you want to marry. Just ask any pizza lover in our house. The box is only important for a minute, and then it's thrown away. For you, it is what is inside that really counts.

The sign said, "Antique Auto Show." My wife and I decided we would take fifteen minutes and stop at this car dealership and look at the antique autos. We were most interested in seeing the ones that went back to when we were young in the fifties and sixties. There was one sleek, black '66 Mustang. It had a flawless exterior and a rich interior. The hood was open so you could look at the horsepower underneath, and sitting on the engine block was a thick book of photos. At the beginning of the photo album, there were "before" pictures of this car. It started as garbage. The first pictures showed a rusted, wrecked, banged-up Mustang. As you look through the book, you could see how the car was slowly transformed step-by-step. It took months, maybe years, of the owner giving patient attention to get this beautiful classic. When the owner saw that wreck, he saw something others didn't see. Let's take a God-moment about . . .

The Rebuilder's Dream

Our word from the Word of God comes from Judges 6. God is looking for a general for His troops who will be a mighty commander and beat the Midianites, who have intimidated and terrorized the Israelites for years. He speaks to Gideon in verse 11. "The angel of the LORD came and sat down under the oak in Ophrah that belonged to Joash the Abiezrite, where his son Gideon was threshing wheat in a winepress to keep it from the Midianites. When the angel of the LORD appeared to Gideon, he said, 'The LORD is with you, mighty warrior.'" Verse 14 says, "The LORD turned to him and said, 'Go in the strength you have and save Israel out of Midian's hand. Am I not sending you?' 'But Lord,' Gideon asked, 'how can I save Israel? My clan is the weakest in Manasseh, and I am the least in my family.' The LORD answered, 'I will be with you, and you will strike down all the Midianites together.'"

Here is Gideon, hiding in a pit. He doesn't look like a mighty warrior at all, and God comes along and says, "Mighty warrior." God didn't see what Gideon was, He saw what he could be and what He intended to make him.

God did the same with Peter. Peter was a flake when he came to Jesus. He was always up and down—inconsistent. Jesus said, "You will be a rock when I am done with you." God

> *When you are dealing with other people, encourage the person God is building in them. You, your friends, your mate, and your children are all in the rebuilding program of Jesus Christ.*

looks at you the same way. He looks at you the way that Mustang owner saw a banged-up car. He sees value, much more than you do. He knows the person He created you to be, and His photo album shows the step-by-step rebuilding.

If you believe how God sees you, then there should be some important changes in how life looks to you. First, when you are down about who you are, look back at the old pictures. Look at who you used to be. You are becoming something. Second, when you are down on yourself, realize you are not finished yet. The Rebuilder is in the process. Third, when you are dealing with other people, encourage the person God is building in them. Tell people what they could be and the good you see in them. Fourth, if you are a parent, don't get hung up on what your child is now. Look at what he could be, and tell him that.

You, your friends, your mate, and your children are all in the rebuilding program of Jesus Christ. Life looks different when we see ourselves and others through Jesus' eyes. We see what we can be. Patiently, step-by-step, the Master is building you into a classic.

S afe Sex" has almost become a national battle cry. We are finally waking up to the fact that sex is out of control in our country, and so we're trying to offer our young people some meaningful guidance, especially in the age of AIDS and sexually transmitted diseases. So we say to them, "Have safe sex." Nowadays, something *married* couples had a hard time talking about—condoms—is now on the front counter in the drugstore.

I have a problem with safe sex. Let's say you have a five-year-old son, and he has a little problem. He likes to play in the middle of the interstate. Well, the parents get together and say, "We have to do something about this. It is not safe to play in the interstate." So they do the only obvious thing they can do. Give him a helmet. That's right. Sure! Now maybe he won't get hurt as badly in the middle of the interstate. Duh! Is that the way to handle it? Has it ever occurred to us that he could stay out of the interstate?! Our kids are not getting the whole story. Well, we will today. Let's take a God-moment about . . .

The Only Safe Sex

Our word from the Word of God comes from 1 Corinthians 6. Verse 13 says, "The body is not meant for sexual immorality, but for the Lord." Verse 18 says, "Flee from sexual immorality. All other sins a man commits are outside his body, but he who sins sexually sins against his own body." There are consequences for taking sex outside of God's boundaries. Some of those consequences are selective. For example, some people get AIDS, but not everybody does. Some people get pregnant, but not everybody does. Some people get sexually transmitted diseases, but not everyone. Those are selective consequences.

Do you know what no one is hearing about today? The universal consequences of sex outside of marriage. Every person who ever uses sex immorally gets three universal consequences, and no condom on earth can protect us against them. Number one: Damaging memories. David said in Psalm 51:3 after his sexual sin, "My sin is always before me." A video camera runs inside your soul and records everything you do with your body, and just when you don't want those images there, in the exclusive love of marriage, the flashbacks come and mar the specialness of that relationship. Nobody tells you about the damaging memories, and you can't shut off the video camera. No condom can protect you against that.

Number two: Lost treasure. Hebrews 13:4 says, "Marriage should be honored by all, and the marriage bed kept pure." Part of the excitement of sex is its uniqueness. "I have never loved anyone this way before. This is a lifetime love, and I've saved this language for you." When you lose the uniqueness, you lose the excitement. Nobody tells you about the treasure you're losing.

And number three: The judgment of God. Again Hebrews 13:4 says, "God will judge the adulterer and all the sexually immoral." You are violating God's laws, and no condom can protect you against that judgment. You think, "Ron, I've already crossed the line." Well, listen to the good news of 1 John 1:9. "If we confess our sins he is faithful and just and will forgive us our sins, and purify us from all unrighteousness." God not only forgives, He cleans you up and restores you.

From today on, keep sex special. Let's give the kids the whole story. With sex outside of God's boundaries, you lose. The only safe sex is saved sex.

The Mississippi River flood of 1993 was a tense time if you had a home or a business near the river in St. Louis. That flood had already done unprecedented damage upriver, and St. Louis was holding its breath. The crests on the Missouri River and the Mississippi River were starting to converge just above the city. Several years earlier, St. Louis had invested heavily in a levee. This levee was bigger than they ever thought they would need. They built it thick and fifty-two feet high, which is many feet above the highest flood crest in the history of the city. Well, this was the five-hundred-year flood. Who knew whether it could get that high? The tension was mounting. The predicted crests were rising over forty feet and toward the fifty-foot mark. Then the moment of truth came. The river crested at incredibly record-high levels but stayed under fifty feet. Well, they were very glad they had built a wall that was strong and high. Let's take a God-moment about how to . . .

Build Your Levee High

Our word from the Word of God comes from Mark 10, which speaks of a flood that is swamping many married people. A deluge of forces are breaking down the walls of marriage. You probably know some couples who have been swept away; maybe you're in one such deluge. Look at Mark 10, beginning at verse 6. Jesus says, "But at the beginning of creation God 'made them male and female.' 'For this reason a man will leave his father and mother and be united to his wife, and the two will become one flesh.' So they are no longer two, but one. Therefore what God has joined together, let man not separate."

This passage makes it clear that God is serious about marriage being for life. If your marriage breaks down, your relationship with God breaks down, and your children are affected too. They are scarred by it. The devil knows that, so he does everything he can to get into your marriage. Today, that flood of forces threatens even the healthiest marriages. Many times both people are working, so they have less time and energy left for each other. The lure of infidelity seems to be more acceptable and justifiable, and it's everywhere around us. There is financial instability. There is the prevalence of divorce, which in turn seems to make it easier for others to get divorced.

That's why God says here, "Guard yourself." Build a flood wall that is high and strong around your marriage. Anticipate all the places the flood could get in, then build a wall against it. For example, schedule regular time to catch up with each other, and make it nonnegotiable so lack of communication is not a hole in the flood wall. How about resentment that builds up when

---

Build a flood wall that is high and strong around your marriage. Anticipate all the places the flood could get in, then build a wall against it.

---

you don't deal with things when they're small? That's why Ephesians 4:26 says, "Do not let the sun go down while you are still angry." Don't stuff your feelings. Those feelings are going to affect your mate. They just won't know what's going on. They won't know why you're acting that way. So deal with issues and feelings when they're small. That's building a flood wall.

What about living in two different worlds? You have to do whatever you must to be together more, even if it means sacrificing financially. Sexual temptation is a hole in the wall. Don't be in any private situation with someone from the opposite sex, and focus all your desires and needs on your mate. Don't even flirt with getting some cheap strokes for your ego from someone of the opposite sex. Look for the places the flood could get into your home, and build a high levee there. There may be a strain on the levee and a few sandbag nights, but if you have built your wall high and strong, your marriage is floodproof.

Missy is the latest member of the Hutchcraft family. She is our Gospel dog. She's a Gospel dog because I keep learning valuable spiritual lessons from her. It is funny to go in the kitchen in the morning and see Missy frozen, looking up at the window. This is her statue routine. When the morning sun streams in from the east, there is a little path of light from the window down to the floor. Missy is hypnotized by that sunbeam, and you cannot get her interested in anything else. When she looks up into that ray of light, she sees dust particles and floating specks dancing around. Now, those particles are always there dancing around, but you can only *see* them when they are in the sunlight. Let's take a God-moment about . . .

Light Vision

Our word from the Word of God comes from John 8:12. The Master is speaking. "When Jesus spoke again to the people, he said, 'I am the light of the world. Whoever follows me will never walk in darkness, but will have the light of life.'" There is no need to stumble if you are in the light. A couple of chapters later in John 11:9–10, He says something similar. "A man who walks by day will not stumble, for he sees by this world's light. It is when he walks by night that he stumbles, for he has no light."

Jesus is talking about what Missy experiences—the ability to see things in the light that we would miss in the dark. When the lights are out, we bump into things in the middle of the night that we wouldn't in the daytime. Now, think about our little dog. She sees things in the light that she can see no other way. So can you. What is really happening in that situation or with that person you've been struggling with becomes clearer when you talk to Jesus about it—because He is the Light. Begin to pray regularly about your struggles, and you will start to understand ways to deal with them that you never saw any other way.

Maybe there's a person you're concerned for, you're struggling with, or you've been hurt by. As you bring them into the light and spend time talking about them, you might see why they are the way they are. Maybe you could do something, or stop doing something, to bring about a breakthrough. How about that situation or that decision? You will get an angle you didn't see before. Maybe you will find a creative solution. I have had one come many times. And the breakthrough always came in the light of Jesus' presence.

Look at the important things and people of your life in the Light. Let Jesus shine on that. Maybe there is confusion right now because you haven't spent enough time in the Light with that issue. Maybe we should all be like Missy, standing fascinated and seeing things in the light we could never see anywhere else.

The passengers were there and the plane was there, but we weren't going anywhere. It was past time to leave, but here were all of us passengers sitting in the flight lounge instead of on the plane and in the air where we belonged. Everybody asked, "What's going on?" Finally, we found out. Our pilot wasn't there. It is very difficult and not advisable to take off without a pilot. He had been on an earlier flight that morning, and we heard he had been delayed and hadn't landed yet. Even though we all had to get somewhere, our pilot was flying something else when we needed him. Let's take a God-moment about . . .

No Pilot, No Progress

Our word from the Word of God comes from 1 Samuel 2. This tells a little about the life of Eli, who was a Jewish religious leader. He had become a priest and was a highly respected man in the nation. Here is the bad news. 1 Samuel 2:12 says, "Eli's sons were wicked men; they had no regard for the LORD." They had been taking advantage of their priestly roles by taking money and resources for themselves from temple offerings. They had been immorally involved with women at the temple. Verse 22 says, "Now Eli, who was very old, heard about everything his sons were doing to all Israel and how they slept with the women who served at the entrance to the Tent of Meeting. So he said to them, 'Why do you do such things? I hear from all the people about these wicked deeds of yours. No, my sons; it is not a good report that I hear spreading among the LORD's people.'" God told Eli that his sons would die, his line would be cut off, and he would no longer be priest. Finally, verse 34 says, "What happens to your two sons, Hophni and Phinehas, will be a sign to you—they will both die on the same day." Tragically, that's just what happened.

Here is a man who is successful in his field, yet his family falls apart. There have been many stories like that, haven't there? Eli demonstrates that it is easy to be taking care of the rest of the world and yet lose your own family. We do not know exactly what the problem was in Eli's home, but being a busy, responsible man suggests that he may have neglected the first congregation—his house. Eventually that cost him everything that mattered. When Eli's family needed him, he was flying something else.

It is easy to be taking care of the rest of the world and yet lose your own family. The pilot belongs first at the controls of his or her plane at home.

Many families are like that. Kids really need Dad and Mom, but parents get increasingly consumed by demands outside the home. Dad gets lost in his business and his kids get lost. He is busy flying his career or some outside interest, so the family is without a pilot. Someone else could be president of the company, and someone else could be manager of that, but you're the only dad and the only husband they have at home. It can happen to a mom, too, especially if she believes the lies that have destroyed our men. For too long, men have believed that working and winning will give them worth, while instead they lose their health and their relationships. Many women now chase the same success phantom that men were fooled by. The other plane you're flying might even be Christian work, where you are over-committed. It can be a hobby, it can be recreation, but the pilot belongs first at the controls of his or her plane at home.

Could it be that your mate and your children are drifting because their pilot is flying something else? Give your family your best, not your leftovers. If you will pilot your family first, God will bless you with more friendly skies.

It is hard to just drive by a Civil War battlefield. I am a history buff, so I like to *stop* at those places. One Civil War battlefield I have frequently driven by is in New Market, Virginia. One time we actually stopped to find out what went on there. In 1864, Ulysses S. Grant was making an all-out push to try to take the Shenandoah Valley in Richmond, the capital of the Confederacy. The Union Army had failed to do that five times before. One part of the army was to move down the Shenandoah Valley, which is where New Market is. General Breckenridge was in charge of some Confederate troops. He was a former vice-president of the United States, and he ordered the students from Virginia Military Institute to march three days to help resist the Union advance. They had not used students before in the army, but these were desperate days. There were many teenagers in that army, and they said, "They'll hear from the Institute today." Well, they did. At a decisive moment in the battle, these kids charged into the Union lines and drove them back. The South won the battle of New Market that day. Let's take a God-moment about . . .

Young People Leading the Charge

Our word from the Word of God comes from Acts 2. God says there will be the greatest outpouring of the Spirit in history taking place just before Jesus comes back. We could be getting close to it. Verse 17 says, "In the last days, God says, I will pour out my Spirit on all people. Your sons and daughters will prophesy, your young men will see visions, your old men will dream dreams." It sounds like young people will help lead the charge in the last great Spirit movement, with old people sharing their vision and cheering them on. If you are young, it is time for you to step up to spiritual responsibility. You've been a taker long enough, drinking in all the Christian stuff. Isn't it time you became a giver? You've gone to meetings long enough.

You need to get a mission, not go to more meetings. You need people you will commit yourself to tell about Jesus, people who will be in heaven because of you. You need to get involved in some needs in your town and in your world that you will start to meet in Jesus' name. This is no time to be sitting around waiting for someone to entertain you in a Christian meeting. You are too old to be spiritually baby-sat, so don't wait for an adult to get kids praying. You do it. Don't wait for an adult to plan an outreach. You do it. Don't wait for an adult to start a Christian club or to start a mission emphasis. You do it.

If you are older than young, be sure you are doing all you can to create a climate and a church where young people are valued, trusted, and challenged. Realize that over two-thirds of the people who ever accept Christ do so by the age of eighteen. The church has no other urgent top-priority mission than its young people, especially the young people around your church who don't even know about Christ yet.

If you are tuned in to the General's final strategy, you will either be a young person on the front lines or an older person encouraging young people to be in spiritual leadership. The most important spiritual battles in history are shaping up right before our eyes, and the outcome may well be determined by young people leading the charge.

It was a little practical joke. Karen and I had just been married, and well, there's great temptation to pull practical jokes on people who just got married. There was a little note that someone put inside our gas cap, and it said, "Have a little fun with this couple. They just got married. Ask them if they just got married, but don't tell them how you know." Well, the only problem is, I found it before we left on our honeymoon. We left it there anyway. It was kind of fun. Of course, the gas station attendants did ask, "Oh, did you just get married?" We had more fun watching the attendants than they did watching us. It's supposed to be a little embarrassing to be newly married and for somebody to be able to tell. Are you able to tell when someone's really happy about being married? Let's take a God-moment about being . . .

Noticeably Married

Our word from the Word of God comes from Ephesians 5, beginning at verse 25. "Husbands, love your wives, just as Christ loved the church and gave himself up for her to make her holy, cleansing her by the washing with water through the word, and to present her to himself as a radiant church, without stain or wrinkle or any other blemish, but holy and blameless." The Bible says here that Christ loves us in a way that ultimately makes us a radiant person without spot, wrinkle, or blemish. And that's also the effect of a husband's sacrificial love for his wife. You can tell a woman who's really being loved and royally treated by her husband. Oh, you don't need a sign to figure it out. She glows. She has a radiance, a confidence, a contentment. That's how God meant it to be. That's what sacrificial love will do for her.

Now, there's the other side of marriage, found in Genesis 2:18. "The LORD God said, 'It is not good for the man to be alone. I will make a helper suitable for him.'" That's the role a real Eve will play in the life of her Adam. You can tell a man whose wife loves like that, who's totally supportive, always loyal, and consistently affirming. You can tell he has a completeness about him. He has a sensitivity. He has nothing to prove. He has a confidence. He's able to care about the needs of other people because his needs are being so lovingly cared for by the woman he loves.

You see, God meant for us to be noticeably married—obviously loved. Something's missing in so many marriages today, isn't it? Instead of creating a glow, it's creating stress. What's

---

You see, God meant for us to be noticeably married—obviously loved. Put him first. Put her first. It sounds risky, but that's the nature of love.

---

missing? Perhaps the missing ingredient is three little words that the minister who married us shared as we left on our honeymoon. He said, "I didn't have time to do marriage counseling. I'm sorry, but I'll give you the three words the minister gave to me on our wedding night. They'll last you the rest of your marriage: Put her first." Or put him first. Now, that doesn't resolve all of the issues, but it sure is a great place to start. I think those are words that most relationships start with but lose when selfishness takes over. Put him first. Put her first. It sounds risky, but that's the nature of love.

Actually, it's riskier to put yourself first. Jesus said, "Whoever tries to keep his life will lose it"—this is a marriage verse—"and whoever loses his life will preserve it" (Luke 17:33). Maybe there's a new beginning for you and the one you pledged your life to in those three words—put him first, put her first. Because you have access to the unconditional love of Jesus Christ, maybe the two of you can be what you may have been in those early married days . . . noticeably married.

Brad is the baby of our family. Today, he is a very big baby in college, but we have one photo we all associate with his childhood. It's our favorite, but it's his unfavorite. He is about two years old, and in our backyard he is standing next to our camping tent that has collapsed on the ground. In one hand, Brad is holding a tent pole about twice his size, and he is holding his other hand against the side of his head, bewildered. He has a pitiful expression that says "What have I done?" He was only playing with a pole, and the whole thing came crashing down. Let's take a God-moment about . . .

Tampering with the Pole That Holds It Up

Our word from the Word of God comes from Malachi 2, beginning at verse 13. "You flood the LORD's altar with tears. You weep and wail because he no longer pays attention to your offerings or accepts them with pleasure from your hands. You ask, 'Why?'" These people are at the altar. They are dedicating their lives. They are rededicating their lives. They are wondering why God is not responding to them. He says, "It is because the LORD is acting as the witness between you and the wife of your youth, because you have broken faith with her, though she is your partner, the wife of your marriage covenant. Has not the LORD made them one? In flesh and spirit they are his. And why one? Because he was seeking godly offspring. So guard yourself in your spirit, and do not break faith with the wife of your youth. 'I hate divorce,' says the LORD God of Israel." The Lord is saying that the lifetime commitment between a man and a woman is the pole that holds up the whole tent. When you remove that pole, it breaks down your relationship with God. It risks the spiritual welfare of a vulnerable child. Keeping those vows is what supports the raising of children who love Jesus. They want to know that the love they came from is still going strong, and when it isn't, they often get lost. Those marriage vows support the church and our culture.

God takes divorce very seriously. Society used to, but not anymore. Within the church at large, the acceptable grounds for divorce are getting wider and wider. And the more accept-

---

Keeping those vows is what supports the raising of children who love Jesus. They want to know that the love they came from is still going strong, and when it isn't, they often get lost. Those marriage vows support the church and our culture.

---

able it becomes, the more likely it is that more people will go to that option. Once the back door is open to marriage, more and more people say, "Well, this is a good time to slip out."

Married or not, let's take divorce as seriously as God does and not find ourselves encouraging a decision that violates God's commitment to marriage. If you are married, make your choice that there is no back door on your marriage. You will not allow an ounce of your energy to go into a possible exit scenario. It is not an option for you. Maybe you need a new start—but in *this* marriage, not another marriage. If you are divorced, know that God hates divorce, but not divorced people. Use your experience to help people heal their marriages, not to end them.

A bewildered little two-year-old guy didn't know what he was tampering with when he removed that tent pole. Don't ever get in the position where you are standing there with a collapse at your feet, saying, "What have I done?" God has made it clear that lifetime marriage holds up most of the things that matter, so your marriage vows and marriage are worth fighting for.

The spotlight in society has fallen on women who choose to have a child—but not a husband. On one hand, the media has been telling the conservative voices to not bother single mothers. On the other hand, I see more and more articles about what happens when there is no father. One of the leading health officers in the United States has said, "The greatest issue facing us is fatherlessness." Isn't that surprising? *Time* magazine commented on women who choose the fatherless family. "They are bringing a child into the world with a hole at the center of his life where a father should be." Let's take a God-moment about . . .

My Father Is Missing

Our word from the Word of God comes from Luke 15. This is the familiar story of the prodigal son, who got his inheritance early from his father, went to a far country and spent it all, and ended up feeding pigs and trying to eat with them. Verse 17 says, "When he came to his senses, he said, 'How many of my father's hired men have food to spare, and here I am starving to death! I will set out and go back to my father and say to him: Father, I have sinned against heaven and against you. I am no longer worthy to be called your son; make me like one of your hired men.' So he got up and went to his father." This is the story of a searching man whose real problem was that he was away from his father.

Maybe that's a picture of you right now. In the story, God is the father, and God has told us He wants us to know Him as heavenly Father. You say, "Well, if He is like the father I had, I'm not too interested." Well, remember this. God is not like the father you had on earth. He is like the father we all wish we had, and what you are feeling down deep in your soul is father lonely. We have a hole we are waiting for a Father to fill. How did we lose Him, and how do we find Him? Look at the verbs in Luke 15. It says that the young man "*set off* for a distant country." The Bible says we have all done that. It says, "We have all sinned and fallen short of God's glorious ideal" and wandered away like sheep. We are away from God by our own choosing. The next verb says he "*squandered* his wealth." All our years away from God are squandered years. They are wasted years until we know the relationship with the Father that we were made for. The next verb, "He *spent* everything." We can do that so easily. In search of the missing part of us, we spend our self-respect, our relationships, our virginity, our reputation, and our future. We cannot find ourselves in achievements, relationships, or pleasure. We spend everything, and then it says, "He *longed* to fill his stomach." Maybe you feel an awful emptiness inside that nothing has been able to fill.

Then we read, "He came to his senses." Maybe that is where God is bringing you right now. It is hard to live without God. It is hell to die without Him. It says that the son went up to his father. There is only one way you can get to the Father you were made by and for. In John 14:6, Jesus says, "I am the way and the truth and the life. No one comes to the Father except through me."

What would happen if you came to Him today? Back in Luke 15, it says that "while he was still a long way off, his father saw him and was filled with compassion for him; he ran to his son, threw his arms around him and kissed him" (v. 20). That is the welcome you could get from God today. He runs to you with His arms open wide. Why don't you run to Him and be born into His family? No longer will you have that hole in the center of your life where a father should be. No earthly father could ever fill that hole anyway. It was made for your heavenly Father. Come to Him, and you will never be Father lonely again.

The "Tripper-Uppers" That Hinder You

That Hinder You

Conquering Your Dark Side

I am basically uncoordinated, but that doesn't mean I can't do anything physical. I can walk, and that is how I get my exercise. It is not all that challenging to put one foot in front of the other and do it as fast as you can. It's a relatively safe way for me to get exercise. No helmet or pads are required, just a few safety rules. Rule one is to walk on the left side of the road. It is not a good idea to have cars come up behind you where you can't see them, especially if you are on hills or curves where *they* might not see *you*. You might end up as a creative new hood ornament. Once, as I was walking on a winding mountain road, cars would suddenly appear around the curve, but I was facing them so I was able to see them before they saw me. It's a good idea to walk facing the traffic. Let's take a God-moment about . . .

Facing What Could Hit You

Our word from the Word of God comes from John 5, beginning at verse 5. Jesus is at the pool of Bethesda, which was supposed to have healing powers, and there are lots of disabled people lying there hoping to get cured. "One who was there had been an invalid for thirty-eight years. When Jesus saw him lying there and learned that he had been in this condition for a long time, he asked him, 'Do you want to get well?'" After the man had responded, Jesus said to him, "'Get up! Pick up your mat and walk.' At once the man was cured; he picked up his mat and walked."

Like the man Jesus healed, we are all in a crippled condition. It may not be physical, but something in our lives holds us back, just as this man was held back for many years by his paralysis. Maybe it's holding you back from the kind of relationships you want to have, from spiritual victory, or from personal peace. It may have been there for a long time—it was thirty-eight years for this man. It's something you can't beat;

it keeps beating you. It's an oncoming car that *keeps* coming at you. It's your personal paralyzer. Maybe it's a habit, a deep hurt, or deep feelings you have stuffed inside for a long time. Maybe it's a sinful stronghold in your personality, and Jesus asks you this curious question, as He did this man, "Do you want to get well?" You've been there so long that maybe you have just accepted this way of being. Or maybe you just deny it, as many Christians do. Maybe you're saying, "Well, Christians don't hate, so I don't hate. Christians don't get bitter, so this isn't bitterness. Christians don't lust, so this isn't lust." Will you call it by its right name? Don't deny it. Maybe you don't want to face it because it would hurt too much or be too hard to change, but it keeps running you over inside.

Do you want to get well? Are you ready to face it if you're not alone? Jesus says, "I am here to fight it with you," just like a little boy who faces the neighborhood bully because his father is with him. It's time to face it before it runs you over for good. First, face it with Jesus, then begin to face it with your mate, your children, your pastor, or a counselor. Get whatever outside help you need. The problem is that as long as it goes unfaced, it is unsurrendered to Jesus. It's not under His lordship. It is a wild, uncontrolled animal inside of you, but He has come to you, saying, "You've lain here long enough. I died to break the power of that thing that has broken you. Open it up to Me. Let Me touch it. Let Me in that dark closet. Let Me give you a new beginning."

Don't turn your back on the oncoming traffic. Face what could hit you. You will be able to walk as you have never walked before, and finally without all that baggage.

Our local high school football team has a history of championships, and the guys work hard to get a starting position. Now, one of the things they do is they spend a lot of time in the weight room. Two of our sons have played for that team, and they'll tell you if you want to be good you sure have to be in that weight room. Of course, it is the best place to lift. For one thing, the coach sees who's working hard. You've also got spotters there—guys who stand by while you're lifting to help get that bar off of you in case you lift more than you can handle. That's what Chris was missing that day. See, he has a weight bench in his basement, and he didn't have anybody around, but he wanted to do his lifting. He was trying to increase the amount that he could bench press . . . all alone. Well, it's not smart to be pushing it when there's no one there to help. He lost it, and all that weight came down on top of him. Chris struggled to finally roll it off him, and he was pretty lucky to escape with only a few bruises. He could have ended up trapped under what he thought he could lift. Let's take a God-moment about . . .

The "I Can Handle It" Trap

Our word from the Word of God comes from 1 Corinthians 10:12–13. It says, "If you think you are standing firm, be careful that you don't fall! No temptation has seized you except what is common to man. And God is faithful; he will not let you be tempted beyond what you can bear. But when you are tempted, he will also provide a way out so that you can stand up under it." If there's a message in those verses, it is this: Do not underestimate temptation, and don't overestimate your strength. See, Chris, our friendly weight lifter, got trapped and was almost crushed because of a common miscalculation: "I can handle it." When it comes to temptation, the devil loves it when we think like that. The words "I can handle this" usually come right before the devil really pins us. Maybe you've already been crushed or trapped by a sin or weakness. You carry the guilt, the shame, the weight, that sense of defeat, and the consequences. Worst of all, you just can't seem to stop. It's like you're a prisoner. Maybe right now you're playing with a compromise, with some wrong thinking, and you're saying, "I can handle it." You have friends you think you can handle without

---

Do not underestimate temptation, and don't overestimate your strength.

---

being like them. You're involved in some physical intimacy that you say you can control. Do you know how many people have lost what they always intended to keep that way? Maybe you're flirting with someone and thinking, even as a married person, "Hey, I'm just playing around. I can handle it." You're hanging around the edges of sin. You're saying, "Well, just a little." You don't ever expect to end up trapped or pinned or hurt. Neither did Chris. But he was. That's why 1 Corinthians 10:12 says, "If you think you are standing firm, be careful that you don't fall!" That arrogance is going to hurt you.

Second Timothy 2:22 says, "Flee the evil desires of youth." It doesn't say resist them, it says avoid them. The devil never tells you where he's going to take you until it's too late. Wherever you are with that temptation, whether you're playing with it or a prisoner to it, it will never be easier to beat it than it is today.

So admit you can't handle it. Give the battle to Jesus. Then choose your exit before you get anywhere close to it. You've underestimated the power of sin to trap you. Don't be a victim of the "I can handle it" trap. You can't handle it, and the Lord has come running into your weight room to warn you not to try it. Listen to His warning and avoid the pain of ending up trapped under what you thought you could handle.

About thirty-five years ago, the world was rocked by the murders of five American missionaries in the jungles of Ecuador. It was front-page news everywhere, and even major photo coverage in *Life* magazine. A young man named Jim Elliot and four others had gone to the Auca Indians, a group of people who were about to kill each other off in their hostility. This was a tribe that one scientist called the worst people on earth. Well, those five young men were martyred, but as a result, the Gospel did get through. Today, virtually that whole tribe knows Christ, partly through the efforts of the missionaries' widows and especially through one of the martyrs' sisters, Rachel Saint. Now, she faced the typical difficulties of trying to translate the Scriptures into another language, but she quickly came across a major problem. The Auca language has no word for *forgive*. You don't ever forgive anyone. If there's a problem, you kill the person. Well, the missionary found a word, and maybe it'll work for you too. Let's take a God-moment about . . .

Shower Power

Our word from the Word of God comes from 1 Corinthians 6:9. "Do you not know that the wicked will not inherit the kingdom of God? Do not be deceived." Then he lists the kinds of people who won't. "Neither the sexually immoral nor idolaters nor adulterers nor male prostitutes nor homosexual offenders nor thieves nor the greedy nor drunkards nor slanderers nor swindlers will inherit the kingdom of God. And that is what some of you [notice the verb] were. But you were washed [there's the shower], you were sanctified, you were justified in the name of the Lord Jesus Christ and by the Spirit of our God."

I saw an interview with some of the Auca men who murdered those missionaries. Today they are serving Christ, and one of them is a native pastor. He said, "We did a terrible thing when we murdered those missionaries, but we know that God has washed our hearts." Do you know, that's how the missionary finally found a way to say the word *forgive* to a culture that had never heard of the word? We had our hearts washed. That's great. A heart that was dirty has been washed. It's finally clean.

Maybe you're ready for a shower today—because you're carrying the weight of guilt for failing your Lord, for going much further sexually then you ever thought, for a habit that has

Maybe you need the feeling of clean, and God has promised it to you, but only because Jesus Christ keeps sin in the past and cleans people in the present.

ruled you for too long, for someone that you've hurt, or for a pattern of lying that continues to haunt you. You know the feeling of dirty.

I was once in a "fight night" in Youth for Christ where, unfortunately, we wasted too much. I wouldn't do it again. The kids got us into this thing at camp where we had to fight each other with chocolate, lard, butter, and eggs. I have never felt so gooey in my life as I did at the end of that. I went into the shower feeling sticky and dirty when I walked in, and I felt so good getting clean. That was shower power.

Maybe you need the feeling of clean, and God has promised it to you, but only because Jesus Christ keeps sin in the past and cleans people in the present. Today, step into God's cleansing shower called forgiveness. When Jesus said, "Father forgive them" on the cross, He was forgiving what you had done. When He said, "It is finished," He meant the bill for your sin. When He said, "My God, my God, why have you forsaken me?" it was so you don't have to be. Leave your sin at His cross. Let Him stamp "forgiven" on your sin, if you will accept Him as your personal Savior. Forgiveness is a new beginning. As the murderers learned so beautifully, when you're forgiven, your heart is washed. You aren't dirty anymore. You are finally clean.

Our friend Ralph is a missionary on the Navajo reservation in Arizona. He was our leader and driver for a week of ministry we had there with a team of young people. One day, we were in a hurry to get to the next meeting. We had a long way to go, and we were driving on a back road shortcut, following a local driver in his pickup truck. Suddenly, that driver made a curious choice. The main road went straight, while the other way went up and around before it reconnected with the main road. Certainly, the main road appeared to be shorter. Ralph said, "I don't know where he's going, but I'm going the shorter way." It seemed to make sense. Well, we went a little farther, but we ended up stopping for a lake that had developed on the road after the last rain. Apparently, the other fellow knew that. We weren't going anywhere except in reverse to get back to where we watched him leave the road. Meanwhile, we saw Mr. Pickup roaring along, passing us on his longer road, and rejoining the main road beyond the puddle while we were still in reverse. Let's take a God-moment about how . . .

The Shortcut Takes Too Long

Our word from the Word of God comes from John 10, beginning at verse 3. Jesus identifies Himself as the Good Shepherd, and He says, "He calls his own sheep by name and leads them out. When he has brought out all his own, he goes on ahead of them, and his sheep follow him because they know his voice." This is a beautiful, tender picture of our relationship with the Lord. It is the intimate relationship between the sheep and the Shepherd.

Maybe several times a week you need to do what I do. I look at Jesus and say, "Me sheep, you Shepherd. Me sheep, you Shepherd." Now, the job description of a sheep is fairly simple—just stay close to the Shepherd. You will never get lost. The problem is that sometimes we think the Shepherd is going too slowly. It's like the pastor whose secretary walked into his office and asked, "Pastor, why are you pacing back and forth like this?" He said, "I'm in a hurry, and God isn't." Do you ever feel like that? Do you know what the greatest enemy of God's best is? Impatience. We are like Ralph. We're behind someone who knows the best way. But we see a way we think will be shorter, so we leave the Lord and go on ahead. When we try to help him out a little bit, eventually we always end up in deep water.

Rebekah was like that in the Old Testament. She knew that God had promised the blessing to her younger son, Jacob. But she could not wait for God to do it His way. She deceived his father, Isaac, who she thought was dying, into giving the blessing to Jacob. It was the right idea, in the wrong way, at the wrong time. It infuriated Jacob's brother, Esau. The result was that the family split up for fourteen years with the brothers hating each other. Rebekah ran ahead of the Shepherd to get to a good goal. Because she rushed it, she ruined it. Maybe you're ahead of your leader right now. You're ahead of the Lord in that relationship. You're running ahead of Him in that business, in those purchases, maybe even in your ministry. You're running ahead of the Lord's pace right now. You're not waiting for God to do it His way and in His time. Ecclesiastes 3:11 says, "He has made everything beautiful in its time." But our rushing is not His time yet. He is getting you ready for the answer, and He is getting the answer ready for you. Don't run ahead of His preparation. Don't run ahead of His provision.

Fellow sheep, one place you don't want to be is on your own, running ahead of your Shepherd. Your idea may seem like a great shortcut to get you there faster, but the shortest road to your answer is God's road, and on God's schedule. Forget the shortcut. It takes too long.

A locking gas cap for your car isn't really that complicated, but don't underestimate my technical ignorance. Karen got one years ago during the oil embargo. That was a time when people were desperate enough to steal gas from your gas tank. So here I am at the gas pump with the key in the gas cap, and I cannot get the dumb thing open. I begin to feel like all the people in the gas station are watching me. I am desperately trying to turn the key and the cap, but nothing is working. I'm muttering, "What is the matter here?! How do you open this thing?" My wife comes up and gently whispers in my ear, "Honey, did you read the instructions?" There they were, right on the gas cap. Me? Embarrassed? I was trying to figure it out, and the instructions were there all along. Let's take a God-moment about . . .

Overlooking the Instructions

Our word from the Word of God comes from Psalm 119, beginning in verse 99. "I have more insight than all my teachers, for I meditate on your statutes. I have more understanding than the elders, for I obey your precepts." The psalmist continues in verses 104–5, "I gain understanding from your precepts; therefore I hate every wrong path. Your word is a lamp to my feet and a light for my path."

How do you know where you are supposed to step next? God says, "Look at My Word. Look at My Book. Look at My instructions." Right here we have practical help about how to figure out what God wants us to do in a given situation. See what the Bible says. You say, "Well, wait a minute. The Bible doesn't mention this person right now. His name is not in the Bible. The Bible doesn't mention this situation. It doesn't really go into detail on this decision." I know many people who pray for guidance and say, "Oh, Lord, what do You want me to do?" They tell me, "Well, the Lord hasn't led me." That is like me trying to figure out that gas cap. We keep making poor choices because we're looking for some specific personal guidance when the instructions are already in print.

Go to the *principles* of God's Word first. You don't need your bedpost to light up at night or get a gurgling feeling inside to lead you. Look for the principles that are already in writing that apply to this situation. You would be amazed at how many answers there are. "Honor your father and your mother" (Exod. 20:12). If you apply that, you might settle a problem. "Do to others as you would have them do to you" (Luke 6:31). How would you like to be treated in this situation? That might settle it. "Be ye not unequally yoked together with unbelievers" (2 Cor. 6:14 KJV). "Love your neighbor as yourself" (Matt. 19:19). "Provide things honest in the sight of all men" (Rom. 12:17 KJV). Only do what is totally honest. "Your body is the temple of the Holy Spirit, so keep it pure" (see 1 Cor. 6:19). "As much as is possible with you, live at peace with all men" (see Rom. 12:18). "If it is within your power to do good, do it" (see Prov. 3:27). *That* verse covers most choices.

God has already spoken, so as you ask, "What should I do, Lord?" He is saying, "I already gave you the instructions. Will you look at My Book?" Knowing God's will is not that hard. It is like opening a locking gas cap. If you quit trying to figure it out on your own and just consult the instructions, you will know what to do.

The night before the Desert Storm troops were to begin their land invasion, trying to liberate Kuwait from Saddam Hussein, a supernatural intervention took place that the troops will never forget. That night there was a sudden shift in the wind. Usually the wind would blow from the north, but it unexplainably shifted to blow from the south. One of the Saudi officers commented, "It never blows from that direction." Well, they can't say *never* anymore.

When the invasion began the next morning, the allied troops witnessed an unbelievable sight. There was a huge, exposed minefield in front of them. Now, those mines had been concealed under the sand and would have destroyed many soldiers, but that unprecedented wind had uncovered the mines so they knew exactly where to step. Let's take a God-moment about . . .

Uncovering the Mines

Our word from the Word of God comes from Hebrews 5:14. "Solid food is for the mature, who by constant use have trained themselves to distinguish good from evil." The ability to distinguish good from evil is called discernment. It is getting tougher and tougher to be able to see sin in disguise and not step on the land mine. Discernment is exactly what our kids need, whether they are kids in your family or in your church. Some of us try to equip them to live in this moral minefield by giving them a list of don'ts for every occasion. But no one can come up with a long enough list to cover everything kids are going to face.

Our world is a moral minefield, and our children are daily going into it. It is easy to be destroyed, to step into something we never meant to. By the time we see the danger, we have stepped on it, and it's too late. It is better to focus on blowing away the sand that covers sin and its consequences. We need to train those we influence, like our children, to be able to distinguish good from evil.

Instead of trying to teach what every moral choice should be, we should teach *how* to make the moral choice. Here are five questions that can expose wrong for what it is. Question number one is, Will it devalue my body? Something is wrong if, in any way, it devalues or degrades this body of mine. Why? Because 1 Corinthians 6:19 says, "Your body is a temple of the Holy Spirit." God lives in that body, and anything you do with that body you drag Him into. So ask yourself, "Will it hurt my body in any way?"

The second question that blows away the sand on the land mines is, Will it let darkness into my mind? Proverbs 4:23 says, "Guard your heart, for it is the wellspring of life." Don't be softened up for an invasion of your mind by letting some dark thoughts and ideas get in there through what you watch or listen to.

The third question is, Will it hurt my reputation? Proverbs 22:1 says, "A good name is more desirable than great riches." Protect your name.

Fourth, Will it hurt the people I influence? Romans 14:13 says, "Make up your mind not to put any stumbling block or obstacle in your brother's way."

The fifth question is, Will it hurt Jesus, who is watching what I'm doing? Ephesians 5:10 says, "Find out what pleases the Lord."

There are land mines in the world that we and our children walk in, and they are covered with bright sand that makes the destructive potential invisible. But God blows away the covering with the wind of His Word. Learn to recognize a moral minefield, and then invade the darkness.

eamwork in marriage really isn't that tough. For example, Karen prepares a meal, and I clear the table and rinse the dishes. I am known as the mad cleaning man around our house. I might clear your plate while you are still in midbite. I like to get my job done. Now, I have had some say to me over the years, "Leave the dishes. Don't worry about them now. Come on into the living room with us. The dishes will wait." Well, I have never known the dishes to rinse themselves or put themselves away. It is a wise discipline to rinse the dirty dishes immediately. Let's take a God-moment about . . .

The Longer It Waits, the Harder It Gets

Our word from the Word of God comes from Ephesians 4:26–27. "In your anger do not sin: Do not let the sun go down while you are still angry, and do not give the devil a foothold." The biblical clock on strained relationships runs out at sundown every day. Remember the old westerns where the marshal says, "You better be out of here by sundown." Well, that is what we are supposed to be saying to any anger, resentment, or conflict that comes up. "Get out of here by sundown."

There is good reason for this. It's like those food remnants on our dirty dishes. If you deal with them right away, they are soft and easy to remove. Just rinse the plate, and the food falls right off. If you wait, it turns hard, so you have to scrape and work because it is stuck. Maybe that is why we call unresolved anger "hard feelings." Anger turns hard quickly, and that gives the devil an opportunity to enter a marriage, a parent-child relationship, a friendship, or a church. At the core of every marriage breakup, probably an issue that was once small was not dealt with immediately. At the core of a broken parent-child relationship, a hurting friendship, a divided church, there are people who didn't clean up their anger when it first appeared and was still small and relatively soft. The devil found his place.

Maybe there is a strained relationship in your life right now. Maybe there have been too many sunsets with bad feelings toward someone. It will never be smaller than it is today. It's probably bigger than it used to be, but this is the smallest it will

---

Today is always your best opportunity to go and do whatever it takes to repair things. The longer you wait, the harder it gets.

---

ever be. This issue will never be easier to address than right now, no matter how hard that might seem. It will only get harder. It will only get more costly. You will only turn darker inside.

Today is always your best opportunity to go to that person and do whatever it takes to repair things. Apologize if you need to, confront if you need to, pray together, and talk it through. You cannot afford the hard spot in your heart that develops from the anger you stuff inside. Anger never stays the same size. Bitterness never stays the same size. They both always grow. Take it from a veteran dish rinser, there is nothing to gain in waiting. The longer you wait, the harder it gets.

The garage sale syndrome. Suddenly, one day this urge hits you. "There's entirely too much stuff in this house. We're going to have a garage sale." Everybody is dispatched to their corner of the house to figure out their contribution. You set up shop, pray for a nice day, and then somebody comes along, likes the price, buys your stuff, and it becomes their stuff. You know, now might be a great time to look at the accumulation around you and do something about it. Let's take a God-moment about . . .

The Unstuffing Adventure

Our word from the Word of God comes from Luke 12, beginning with verse 24. Jesus says, "Consider the ravens: They do not sow or reap, they have no storeroom or barn; yet God feeds them." What an interesting concept of security. He said, "No storeroom." In verse 30 Jesus continues: "For the pagan world runs after all such things, and your Father knows that you need them. But seek his kingdom, and these things will be given you as well. Do not be afraid, little flock, for your Father has been pleased to give you the kingdom. Sell your possessions and give to the poor. Provide purses for yourselves that will not wear out, a treasure in heaven that will not be exhausted, where no thief comes near and no moth destroys. For where your treasure is, there your heart will be also."

Jesus says here that putting His agenda first means "unstuffing." This means looking at all I've accumulated and asking, "Now, what could I do without?" and giving it away to make a difference. This is giving for the love of Jesus. Hudson Taylor, the great pioneer missionary to China, wrote in his book *To China with Love* these words that really challenge me. He was meditating on the Lord's return and wrote, "The effect of this blessed hope was a thoroughly practical one. It led me to look carefully through my little library to see if there were any books there that were not needed or likely to be of further service, and to examine my small wardrobe, to be quite sure that it contained nothing that I should be sorry to give an account of should the Master come at once. The result was that the library was considerably diminished, to the benefit of some poor neighbors, and to the far greater benefit of my own soul, and that I found I had articles of clothing also which might be put to better advantage in other directions. . . . I have never gone through my house, from basement to attic, with this object in view, without receiving a great accession of spiritual joy and blessing."

I said to Karen, "Honey, I think this needs to be the year of divesting for us." Simplifying our lives so God could lead us any way and anywhere He wants. I don't want Him to come someday and ask me to do something and I say, "I can't. Look at all my stuff." I don't want Him to come back someday and say, "What are you doing with all that stuff you're sitting on? It could have been put to use." Hudson Taylor wrote, "I believe we are all in danger of accumulating—it may be from thoughtlessness, or from pressure of occupation—things which would be useful to others, while not needed by ourselves, and the retention of which entails loss of blessing. If the whole resources of the Church of God were well utilized, how much more might be accomplished! How many poor might be fed, and naked clothed, and to how many of those as yet unreached the Gospel might be carried!"

He certainly caught the spirit of the verses we just read. Maybe we're guilty of the sin of accumulating. Maybe it's time to sacrifice more so someone else can have just enough. In fact, it's quite a family adventure to do this together—to gather up your stuff and deliver it to people who need it or agencies that can get it to them. Look around you. It's all earth stuff, but when you give it to the Master, and give it to people who really need it, you convert earth stuff into heaven treasure.

There is an unforgettable drive along the Hudson River just north of New York City. Along the way is a place called Storm King Mountain, and it is a foreboding, impressive mountain peak. This ribbon of highway clings to the edge of the mountain high above the Hudson River, and what a panorama it is. I have always been fascinated with a castle that's on an island in the middle of the river. It looks like a strong fortress, maybe something from Robin Hood. My wife and I once had an opportunity to cruise up the Hudson River, so we cruised right past that island and got a close-up. As I talked with the captain in the wheelhouse, he said, "That's called Bannerman Island and Bannerman Castle." He explained that Mr. Bannerman had been an arms dealer with all kinds of people over the years. Little sentry towers still rise from the water around the island, and there are lots of stories about people coming and going for weapons through several wars. In the sixties, an explosion closed the business. And the castle? I was surprised to learn the truth about the castle. That castle is impressive on the outside, but it is gutted on the inside. It has no beams, no supports, and the roof is open. It is totally hollow. In fact, it is rotting and could collapse at any time. Let's take a God-moment about being . . .

Hollow on the Inside

Our word from the Word of God comes from Matthew 23, beginning at verse 25. Here is what Jesus said of certain people in His day. He said to the Pharisees, "You clean the outside of the cup and dish, but inside they are full of greed and self-indulgence. Blind Pharisee! First clean the inside of the cup and dish, and then the outside also will be clean. Woe to you, teachers of the law and Pharisees, you hypocrites! You are like whitewashed tombs, which look beautiful on the outside but on the inside are full of dead men's bones and everything unclean. In the same way, on the outside you appear to people as righteous but on the inside you are full of hypocrisy and wickedness."

Jesus is describing people who look great on the outside, but they have serious problems on the inside. This could be true of a church, an organization, or a leader. It could be you or me. We live in a world where image and appearance are everything, so we work on our fitness, hair, and wardrobe; make good impressions; act like we have it all together; but maybe

---

"There's a darkness inside me that scares me." Let Jesus into that darkness.

---

there is another us. When we're alone and thinking, we can feel the emptiness. We can't explain it, but we can't deny it. Beneath the image, we know the darkness. We know the sin. We know the struggle. As one person said to me, "There's a darkness inside me that scares me." There is a sense that if it's not dealt with, we will eventually collapse.

Listen to Jesus. In John 8:12 He gives an encouraging answer. "I am the light of the world. Whoever follows me will never walk in darkness, but will have the light of life." Let Jesus into that darkness and into that emptiness. He says to you, "I've tried so long to get in. Will you let Me in to that emptiness and that darkness?" That drives us to the One who knows all about it, the One who sees past our image. It should bring you, not to depression, but to the cross. Say to Him, "Lord, I've been trying to cover up the pain inside, and the sin, but I need to clear it up. I'm not what I appear to be. You know that. No more trusting in me. I need You."

Jesus builds people from the inside out, so there is no more empty castle. With Jesus inside, you will no longer have to deal with the hollowness in your heart.

This is embarrassing to tell, but I had a hole in my pants the other day, and I didn't know it. I was traveling with some of my coworkers on an airplane, and I was making the rounds up and down the aisle, visiting with each one. Suddenly I heard, "Ron . . . Ron," behind me. And I was given the unwelcome news about the hole in my pants. I was embarrassed, but I needed to know it. And yes, I sat down for the rest of the trip. Let's take a God-moment about . . .

The Good Way
to Get Bad News

Our word from the Word of God comes from Proverbs 27:17. It says, "As iron sharpens iron, so one man sharpens another." In the King James Version it says, "Iron sharpeneth iron; so a man sharpeneth the countenance of his friend." A friend will love you enough to tell you the truth, even if it is unwelcome truth. These are things that will sharpen and improve you. Did you ever go for hours with something out of place and no one told you? You ask, "Why didn't someone tell me?" It's important to hold up a mirror for someone that you love to see what they look like. You love them enough to say, "Look, this is what you look like right now."

We have to be willing to *receive* love from someone holding up a mirror too. This doesn't mean just critical stuff. We mirror each others' strengths, successes, and pluses, saying, "Honey, look at yourself. Look what you have going for you." We need to also care enough to say, "You look good, but there is this hole I thought you should know about." Maybe it's a hole in the way you treat people, in something you've been neglecting, and you don't even realize it. Maybe it's a hole in your integrity, your character, or your walk with God. Are you open to loving criticism from other people? Are you approachable? Will you let them tell you? Are you just going to go on and on with that hole in your life because you won't listen to someone who loves you? "I don't want to hear it" doesn't make it untrue. You need iron to sharpen iron so you can be a more whole person.

Maybe God has been trying to speak to you through your mate or your parent, and they tell you some things you don't want to hear, but you need to listen to that. It might be hard for you, as a parent, to look in a mirror that's being held up by

---

Listen to someone who cares enough to tell you that there is a hole in your life.

---

your son or daughter. You don't want to hear this from them. You're supposed to be their teacher, but sometimes they turn out to be ours. Or maybe it's through a friend, a pastor, or worse yet, someone who isn't even a friend at all. But it's the truth. Maybe the criticism isn't even being tactfully or lovingly said, but it could still be truth you need to hear.

Could it be that God has been trying to confront you with a fatal flaw for a long time? His Holy Spirit has been trying to get your attention, and you've drowned Him out? Maybe you have quenched the Spirit, run from Him, rationalized the truth, covered it up, and stayed busy. Today is your day to turn and face this loving Father. He loved you enough to sacrifice His own Son for you, so you need to say to Him, "Father, You're right, and I've run from it long enough. I need to deal with this weakness. I need to deal with this fatal flaw, and today I face it, and I'm surrendering it to You for Your touch."

Listen to someone who cares enough to tell you that there is a hole in your life. It hurts to hear about it, but it hurts more not to hear about it, and even more if you don't deal with it. Having someone love you by confronting you is really the good way to get bad news.

Sports give us a lot of thrills and occasional tragedies, like the death of the captain of the Boston Celtics basketball team, Reggie Lewis. After he collapsed in a basketball playoff game, a team of doctors said he had a potentially dangerous heart condition, and he couldn't play anymore. He went for a second opinion, and those doctors said he had a much less serious condition and could gradually return to playing. Well, he died doing some practice shooting in a gym a few months later, maybe trying to make a comeback. One newscaster reported it this way, "He heard what he wanted to hear." This shocking death of Reggie Lewis raised a larger medical debate in the press. They call it doctor shopping. Basically, you keep asking around until someone tells you what you want to hear. Let's take a God-moment about . . .

When Shopping Costs Too Much

Our word from the Word of God comes from 1 Kings 12. It is the beginning of the reign of King Rehoboam, Solomon's son, in Israel. The people are asking that he be a little easier on them than his father was, and he is trying to figure out what to do. First, he goes to the elders, and the elders who had served King Solomon tell him that if he is a servant to the people, they will gladly serve him. Then he says, "I think I will talk to my young friends," so he talks to his peers. They say to him, "Hey, flex your muscle there, King Rehoboam. Tell them you're going to be tough. Let them know who is in charge."

First Kings 12:8 says, "Rehoboam rejected the advice the elders gave him and consulted the young men who had grown up with him and were serving him." Verse 13 says, "The king answered the people harshly. Rejecting the advice given him by the elders, he followed the advice of the young men." Verse 19 reveals the outcome. "So Israel has been in rebellion against the house of David to this day." He lost an awful lot. Why?

Because he shopped for the advice he wanted to hear and not for the truth. He wanted advice that would reinforce him, not challenge him. So he shopped until he got a green light because he had already decided he wouldn't obey a red light.

That is a lot like us. Chances are, God has put someone in our lives, and maybe several someones, who tell us the truth, whether we like it or not. But because we're insecure, we shop for someone who will just agree and support what we decide to do. Rehoboam took the appealing advice, and it doomed his kingdom.

The Bible encourages us to check our ideas by seeking out godly advisers who will tell us the truth. Go with a blank sheet of paper, not an opinion you just want them to sign. The truly wise person is the one whose decisions look good ten years from now, and not just ten days from now. That person seeks the advice of a parent, of someone who has been down this road, and of people who walk with God. Ultimately, the smart course is to measure every choice by the Word of God. Don't try to Scripture shop for verses that just support what you want. Honestly put your ideas and your life next to God's statements on the subject, and do what God says, not what you like.

If you have been doctor shopping to justify what you are doing, you're on the Rehoboam road—a road where you lose what you were scheming to keep. Go looking for the truth, even if it hurts, and not for strokes. Go looking for the voice of God, maybe through a human adviser. You cannot afford shopping for what you want to hear. It costs entirely too much.

When I was unpacking in a hotel room once, I flipped on the television, and it automatically came on to the adult movie channel. I switched immediately, and later when I turned it off, I left it on the news channel I had been watching. I thought, "Okay, I have this thing figured out. The next time the TV comes on, it will come on to the news channel." Wrong. That TV was programmed to always come on to the sleazy channel. Let's take a God-moment about how . . .

The First Channel
Is the Worst Channel

Our word from the Word of God comes from 1 Peter 2:9–10. "You are a chosen people, a royal priesthood, a holy nation, a people belonging to God, that you may declare the praises of him who called you out of darkness into his wonderful light. Once you were not a people, but now you are the people of God." Verse 11 says, "Dear friends, I urge you, as aliens and strangers in the world, to abstain from sinful desires, which war against your soul."

The message is clear. Stay away from sinful desires if you are one of the people of God. This is not easy to do in our world. Wherever you go these days, our world seems tuned to the bad channel. The temptation to think sinfully about the opposite sex is everywhere. There it is on a billboard. There it is in an ad for a bad show in the middle of a good show. There it is in a catchy song or in a sexual scene in a movie that is otherwise pretty decent. It's on a magazine cover or the covers of videos at the video store. Sometimes, maybe you don't find it so accidentally. Maybe sometimes you choose the lust channel, intentionally looking at the wrong things or listening to things that are dirty. Face it, the lust channel is on all day long, whenever provocatively dressed women parade by. You ask, "What about men?" Well, men tend to struggle more with lust, but it can go either way.

Jesus hasn't changed His mind about it. He said in Matthew 5:28, "Anyone who looks at a woman lustfully has already committed adultery with her in his heart." Aren't you tired of losing to lust? Haven't you had enough cheap thrills followed by the feelings of shame, guilt, and defeat? That is why Peter says, "Abstain from sinful desires, which war against your soul."

Are you ready to win? You have to play defense and offense if you want to win this one. Defense says, don't get anywhere near it. Abstain. Realize that every time you allow yourself to take another lust look, you delay victory at least one more day. The look doesn't take long, but the impression in your soul lasts much longer. It wars in your soul, doesn't it? Every lust look feeds a monster you're trying to kill. You cannot afford to give any more ammunition to the enemy that has defeated you so many times, so you need to print in bold letters on your heart, "It's just not worth it." A lust look takes you farther from God and makes you less satisfied with the one you're married to and more ashamed of yourself. Train your eyes to look away instantly, to keep your eyes only in righteous places, and give your mental TV another channel to switch to. That's playing offense.

Psalm 119:11 says, "I have hidden your word in my heart that I might not sin against you." Memorize verses from God's Word, and when you think sin, immediately switch channels and hear that verse. Every day, we walk into a room where the channel is already on the sinful stuff. Before we ever turn on the screen, we have to make the deliberate choice that it is *our* TV, and we will not keep it on a channel that leads only to darkness. The lust channel isn't worth it. Learn to develop the fastest switching hand in the west, and turn quickly from the lust channel to the Lord channel. That's no-regrets viewing.

On the north side of Chicago, the old amusement park is gone, but the memories of going there as a boy are still around. I remember one ride called the Rotor. It was like a giant washing machine tub, except they didn't put clothes in it. People were the clothes. We would step into this big, round cylinder and stand on a ledge. It would start to spin, getting faster and faster, and then the floor would drop out from underneath us. You could hear the screams halfway across the city as we were thrown against the outer edges. Centrifugal force is amazing. The faster things are spinning, the more things are spun to the edge. Let's take a God-moment about being . . .

Spun to the Edge

Our word from the Word of God comes from Luke 10:38–42. "As Jesus and his disciples were on their way, he came to a village where a woman named Martha opened her home to him. She had a sister called Mary, who sat at the Lord's feet listening to what he said. But Martha was distracted by all the preparations that had to be made. She came to him and asked, 'Lord, don't you care that my sister has left me to do the work by myself? Tell her to help me!' 'Martha, Martha,' the Lord answered, 'you are worried and upset about many things, but only one thing is needed. Mary has chosen what is better, and it will not be taken away from her.'"

Martha is spinning in this story, and she is spinning so fast that she spins Jesus right to the edge. Martha has a lot of children, and I think I'm one of them. Could it be that your life has become so busy that you are neglecting Jesus? You don't mean to, and you never meant to. The irony of Martha's story, and maybe yours and mine, is that we are busy serving Jesus. We're not out doing bad things. We're out doing His work, but Martha has Jesus right in her home, and she misses Him. In fact, the phrase "distracted by all the preparations" literally means "pulled away." She was saying, "Jesus, I'd like to be with You, but hold it. Have you seen my to-do list? Have you heard all I have to do? I have to take care of the roast. Oh, there goes the phone again."

The old song says, "The longer I serve Him, the sweeter He grows." For that to be true, we have to be sitting at Jesus' feet. Maybe you have noticed lately that the work you used to do out of devotion is now duty. It used to come from your passion for Jesus, and now it's just a profession. You're cranking it out for Jesus, but there's no real joy. There's no real fulfillment. You're suffering from the results of spiritual centrifugal force, and everything is going to remain frustrating and stressful until you put first what Jesus called "what is better." The better portion, the better part, He says, "is to sit down and be with Me."

Why don't you make your time with Jesus a nonnegotiable in your schedule? It is noncancelable. No one can have that time. Start to write a journal again about your times with Jesus. And don't just read the Bible to be with a book. Be with Jesus. Put that Book in your lap, and say, "Jesus, this is Your letter to me. Speak to me as if You're sitting in the chair right there across the room from me." Then in prayer, walk through all the details of your day with Him before you ever live them. Stay in close, frequent touch all day long. Loving Jesus is more important than serving Jesus.

If you're spinning so fast that Jesus is on the edge, you're living in the barrenness of a busy life. Get off your feet for awhile and sit at His.

When you're outside on a warm night, you expect bugs, so you play defense. You put spray on, swat bugs, and spray the yard. Now, you don't expect to wear bug spray and sit with a swatter when you're indoors, right? Bugs belong outside, but sometimes I find myself being dive-bombed, buzzed, or bitten by some winged critter when I'm inside. I could spend the rest of the season swatting, or I could find the place those critters are getting in. So when you go to our screen door in the back, you will find a little piece of Kleenex stuffed in a little hole. We are fighting them at the point of entry. Let's take a God-moment about . . .

Find the Hole and Plug It

Our word from the Word of God comes from Ephesians 4:27. "Do not give the devil a foothold." First Peter 5:8 tells us that the devil is like a lion seeking someone to devour. He's not particular. He just goes after anyone who is not alert or aware or who has their guard down. He's looking for a spiritual lunch, and he'd love it to be you. Once he is in, he bites and devours, and you're in for a real battle to swat him away. This verse from Ephesians, though, suggests the place to fight him is at the point of entry. Don't let him in. James 4:7 says, "Resist the devil, and he will flee from you." If you will just resist him, and block his entry, he will go away.

Your job is to find the weak spot in your life that the enemy can exploit. If you were the devil, what would you look for? Don't do anything careless that might give your enemy something to work with. Do not give the devil a foothold. He only needs a small compromise to come in and do large damage. He'll drive a truck through that little compromise you gave him to work with. Watch for the little anger that you don't resolve quickly. Watch for the little flirting with a sin that you should be fleeing in the first place. Maybe your weak spot or the low point in the wall is the way you handle money, conflict, or the truth, especially when you're in a jam. Maybe it's the way you handle your temper, the opposite sex, or how you are when you don't get your way. Maybe it's how you handle disappointment or depression.

See, every coach identifies the weakness in the other team so he can exploit that weakness. Every general identifies the

---

If you were the devil, what weak spot in your life would you exploit? Begin every day saying, "Dear Lord, I give you my weak spot."

---

weakness in the other army so he can exploit that weakness. Well, that's just what Satan does. He did it to Jesus when He was in the wilderness during that time of temptation. Jesus had not eaten for forty days, so the devil went for Jesus' vulnerable spot—hunger.

Please honestly finish this sentence: Right now, the vulnerable spot in my life is . . . Okay, now it could be a legitimate need that you may be tempted to meet with something other than God's best. Your mission is to plug the hole the devil can use. How? First, with daily prayer. Begin every day in its early waking moments saying, "Dear Lord, I give you my weak spot. I give you my vulnerable spot. I crown You Lord of it." Then there is that daily surrender when you turn it over to Him and say, "Lord, the battle is Yours." Third, there is daily wall building. Begin to build your day so that you are stronger in that area, and plan ahead so the devil cannot get in there. Don't even give him an opportunity. When you leave an opening, not only do bugs come in, but in this case, a lion comes in. You can keep battling the intruder and feeling the bites, or you can plug that hole.

Missy's doing it again. She is our young dog who loves playing with bubbles. She loves to chase bubbles that we blow onto the floor. And it's fun to watch. Now, she also loves bottles. She enjoys a good battle with any two-liter, plastic soda pop bottle. When she attacks that thing, you can hear it all through the house. She tosses it in the air, forces it up against the wall, and thuds it along the floor. She fights it until she's totally exhausted, then suddenly you hear her plop on the kitchen floor. She has worn herself out in combat with a dumb plastic bottle. Let's take a God-moment about . . .

Plastic Wars

Our word from the Word of God comes from Luke 17, beginning at verse 26. "Just as it was in the days of Noah, so also will it be in the days of the Son of Man. People were eating, drinking, marrying and being given in marriage up to the day Noah entered the ark. Then the flood came and destroyed them all. It was the same in the days of Lot. People were eating and drinking, buying and selling, planting and building. But the day Lot left Sodom, fire and sulfur rained down from heaven and destroyed them all. It will be just like this on the day the Son of Man is revealed."

Was there something terribly wrong about eating, drinking, marrying, planting, building, buying, and selling? Those things are not patently wrong, but God is saying that they were living in important times, with important battles to fight, and meanwhile, they were trapped in the everyday trivia of life. They were fighting with plastic bottles, getting all worn out and stressed out, while life-and-death battles were left unfought. Sounds like many of us. Some of us are so consumed by our business, by our career, by the pursuit of success, and by the survival of life that we end up seeking last the kingdom of God.

We have little time left to do God's work, to build relationships with lost people, to get involved in presenting Christ to our dying world. Too many Christians are caught up in fighting microbattles while we are losing the macrobattles for people's ever-living, never-dying souls. We fight over denominational distinctives and the 10 percent that divides us instead of the 90 percent that unites us. We split hairs over the don'ts of the Christian life until we are known more for what we are against rather than who we are for. We get lost in doctrinal disputes while a world that couldn't care less about them goes to hell. Some of us are pretty aloof from other believers because we are more spiritual than they are—by our definition of spirituality. Some of us are getting all worn out on plastic wars, fighting fiercely over issues that make us miss the dying people all around us.

Now, doctrine is important, and righteous behavior is important. But we dare not lose sight of the greatest battle of all, which is the battle for lost souls. Let's not be so busy purifying the faith, making sure that every *i* is dotted and every *t* is crossed that we lose our focus on bringing multitudes to Christ. We cannot afford to fight each other, or a plastic bottle, when a life-and-death war rages all around us.

If you shoot a gun or a bow, you know what you want to hit. You want to hit the bull's-eye. Now, if you're in a battle, it isn't quite as easy to know where the bull's-eye is. Well, Daniel Morgan knew. Daniel Morgan commanded a unit called Morgan's Raiders during the Revolutionary War, on the colonists' side. He made a decisive difference, especially at the battle of Saratoga, which many scholars say was the turning point of the Revolutionary War. Morgan told his riflemen where their bull's-eye was in the battle. He said, "Forget the poor fellows who fight for six pence a day. Concentrate your fire on the epaulet men." Epaulets are those fringe decorations that officers used to wear on their shoulders. As a result of Morgan's orders, British General Burgoine's officer ranks were so depleted that he surrendered at Saratoga. Well, Morgan's strategy is still the way to win a battle. Let's take a God-moment about . . .

The Target on Your Back

Our word from the Word of God comes from Luke 22, beginning with verse 31. Jesus is anticipating the intense spiritual warfare Simon Peter will go through as Jesus is arrested, tried, and crucified. "Simon, Simon, Satan has asked to sift you as wheat. But I have prayed for you, Simon, that your faith may not fail. And when you have turned back, strengthen your brothers." Jesus knows what kind of war Peter is about to be in, so He says, "I'm going to pray for you because I see that you are going to be one of My great leaders." Satan is not omnipresent. He has to be selective in his targets, so he says, like Daniel Morgan of old said, "Go for the leaders." The minute you step up to making a difference for Jesus, you step into the devil's sights. That's not a reason to be afraid. Nothing can reach a target that is protected by the blood of Jesus Christ. I know a leader in the Christian movement who's been in great turbulence. One of his board members said to him, "You know what I think you ought to do? Why don't you just get a nice, fat, juicy job in corporate America and get the target off your back?" I'm sure he was being facetious, but his point was well taken. The target is on the back of a leader.

I see two groups here. First of all, there are those in leadership. Maybe you're in a group that is exercising leadership for the Lord, whether on a small scale or on a large scale. Don't be surprised if you're drawing fire, but remember to fight it as a spiritual battle. Don't fight human beings, human forces, and economic forces. Fight this as a spiritual battle, and live carefully. Don't do anything that could give Satan something to work with. Anticipate all the ways he could bring you down, trap you, restrict you, and then, build your life in such a way that he couldn't do that. Build a high wall at those points.

Maybe you're in the second group. Maybe you're around a spiritual leader, benefitting from him. Don't let any bullets come from *you*. We're supposed to pray, as Jesus did, for a spiritual leader. He said, "I'm going to pray for you, because I know Satan wants you because you're going to be a leader." Don't ever be one who wounds a man or a woman God is using, who's already a target. Be a spiritual bodyguard for the leaders you know. Get between them and the enemy bullets with your prayers. Be part of the spiritual security force. Pray intensely for the leader you know. Let's protect each other, let's pray for each other, and don't be discouraged if the devil takes aim at you. It means that hell considers you a threat because heaven is about to use you.

everal years ago I had the privilege of visiting Old Jerusalem, and as I walked through the city, I saw a curious sight. I saw some Israeli soldiers who appeared to be on holiday because they had their arms around their girls, and they were laughing and shopping. The curious part was that each one had a gun strapped over his shoulder—an Uzi, with a full clip of ammunition. Those Israeli soldiers knew they always needed to be prepared for war, even when they were taking the day off. Let's take a God-moment about . . .

Never
without Your Weapon

Our word from the Word of God comes from Psalm 119, the longest chapter in the Bible. It is appropriately devoted to the power of the Word of God. Verse 9 says, "How can a young man keep his way pure?" You may or may not be young, but I'm sure you've asked that question. How can I win over this temptation? Here's the answer. "By living according to your word." Then the psalmist says, "I seek you with all my heart; do not let me stray from your commands." Lord, I really want to do the right thing, but sometimes I get off on a detour. Now, here's the strategy for winning that battle. "I have hidden your word in my heart that I might not sin against you" (v. 11). Here David is talking about memorizing the words of God from the Bible, making them part of your personality. That's the weapon we use to fight sin and temptation.

You say, "I read the Bible." No, this is talking about knowing the Bible by heart, memorizing it. I have memorized Ephesians 6:10–18, that great spiritual warfare passage, and many mornings—as I've been getting ready or haven't been feeling all that great or have been facing some gloomy prospects or a heavy load—I've quoted that passage. And many times, it has turned the spiritual tide. D. L. Moody said, "When you think sin, think Scripture." You can't do that if you don't have Scripture buried in your personality by memorization. You can't always reach for your Bible, but you can reach in and pull up whatever you've made part of you. This is like portable spiritual power, wrapped up in Scripture committed to memory.

Now, if you haven't been consciously, consistently committing verses to memory, you're spiritually a lot weaker than you need to be. Learn some of the promises of God to stand on in those moments when worry is winning. Memorize Psalm 55:22, for example. "Cast your cares on the LORD and he will sustain

---

Memorize the words of God from the Bible, making them part of your personality. That's the weapon we use to fight sin and temptation.

---

you; he will never let the righteous fall." I've sent that verse to the door many times when worry's been knocking. Learn His promises to fight temptation, like 1 Corinthians 10:13. "No temptation has seized you except what is common to man. And God is faithful; he will not let you be tempted beyond what you can bear. But when you are tempted, he will also provide a way out so that you can stand up under it." Try James 4:7, "Resist the devil, and he will flee from you." Memorize that passage in Ephesians 6. Learn the warnings of Scripture to fight when sin looks inviting. For example, James 1:15 says, "Then, after desire has conceived, it gives birth to sin; and sin, when it is full-grown, gives birth to death." All of a sudden, sin is revealed as the killer it really is. Write those verses on a card that you want to memorize. Learn them by a handle. Put a title on them—temptation, worry, or whatever you want to use as your subject matter. Keep the card in places where you frequently go, and review, review, review. Try it on as many people as you can.

Those Israeli soldiers have won the respect of the world. That day in Jerusalem, I saw one reason why. They know something that every follower of Christ has to remember. We must always be prepared for war, and it doesn't stop because you are relaxing, so always carry your weapon—the loaded artillery of God's words in your heart.

I once saw a package hanging on a novelty rack that said "Temporary Tattoos." I didn't think those words went together, but these are stickers that you just rub on your arm. I have also seen a Norman Rockwell sketch from World War II, with a sailor who has a tattooed list of girls' names all over his muscular arm. Apparently one had been added at a time because it says "Gretchen," then her name is crossed out, then "Francine" crossed out, and then "Sophia" crossed out. There are about five or six names like that. Finally, you see the name of the girl who apparently was his current interest—she didn't have a line through her name. Of course, you wonder how long that name was going to be there before it had a line through it too. You can cross a relationship off your arm, but it isn't that easy to cross it off your heart. Let's take a God-moment about . . .

Erasing Tattoos

Our word from the Word of God comes from Psalm 51:1–3. David is experiencing grief and regret over his adulterous relationship with Bathsheba, to whom he is now married. He says, "Have mercy on me, O God, according to your unfailing love; according to your great compassion blot out my transgressions. Wash away all my iniquity and cleanse me from my sin. For I know my transgressions, and my sin is always before me." Now, David didn't know anything about video recorders, but he had one in his soul. Everybody does. See, what people never tell you about sex before or outside of marriage is that when you are making love, you're making memories, and when you're sinning, that recorder is always rolling. As David said, "My sin is always before me. Lord, I need Your forgiveness." God had forgiven him, but the memories continued to roll on. The pleasures of a night can turn into the guilt and regret of a lifetime. Author and speaker Josh McDowell met a man who said to him, "I've not been able to be alone in bed with my wife for over ten years. There is always someone else there." Josh said, "What do you mean?" He said, "There's all the memories of all the other women. I don't want them there, but they keep replaying." Sin leaves tattoos on your heart and your mind. Remember that as you feel the strong pull of temptation. Calculate the cost of your sin first, and include this memory factor. Tattoos are hard to erase.

There is good news. Acts 3:19 says, "Repent, then, and turn to God, so that your sins may be wiped out, that times of refreshing may come from the Lord." You say, "Is it too late for me after what I've done?" No, because God is in the business of erasing the tattoos of sin. But that seldom happens overnight. The blood of Jesus, shed to pay for that sin, is so strong that over time it can begin to dim the impression sin has left. Ask Jesus to wash your memories daily after you've repented of that sin. If you did that for a year, there would be 365 layers of Christ's daily grace over the tattoos of your sin, and that makes a difference. If you have sinned sexually, repent and surrender that sin to Him, and from that moment on, this powerful Savior begins to restore your spiritual and emotional virginity. He will make the innocent expressions of love special once again. Sin makes a powerful impression on the human soul and on your memory, just like a tattoo. Think about that before you let temptation steal a clean conscience for a few moments of sinful pleasure. There is no such thing as a temporary tattoo.

If you live on the East Coast, one word is sure to get your attention: Hurricane. Hurricane Hugo was one of those mega-storms that really got our attention. You could watch the news for several nights before Hugo arrived, and they would show you a cyclonic circle inching across the weather map toward an uncertain destination. Half a million people were evacuated, from Florida to the Carolinas, not knowing where that little circle on the map was going to land. Finally, it became clear that Hugo's 130-mile-an-hour winds would slam ashore at Charleston, South Carolina. The challenge for public officials was to convince everyone that it was time to move. The mayor gave a solemn warning to the people there. He said, "Hugo is a killer. If you stay, you may very well die." That was true then, and it is true now. Let's take a God-moment about . . .

Dying from Doing Nothing

Our word from the Word of God comes from the prophet Ezekiel in the Old Testament, chapter 18, beginning at verse 30. "Repent! Turn away from all your offenses; then sin will not be your downfall. Rid yourselves of all the offenses you have committed, and get a new heart and a new spirit." God asks a pointed question, "Why will you die?" Then He turns it around and says, "Repent and live." In the Bible, the word *repent* always refers to changing your mind about sin. Whatever you have been coddling and tolerating in your life, turn your back on it, change your mind about God, and pin all your hopes on Him.

Sin, like Hurricane Hugo, is a killer. With a hurricane, those who don't leave might survive. But when it comes to sin, there are no survivors. If you die without your sins forgiven, you will never see God's presence. You will be lost forever, separated by the sin He wanted to forgive because of what Christ did on the cross. Not only are there eternal consequences of not dealing with our sin, but sin also kills now. It blows apart marriages, damages the people you love with your temper, mars the beauty and purity of sex, destroys your reputation, and makes your emotions dark and depressed.

People who die in a hurricane don't have to do anything to be killed by it. Many of them die from doing nothing and just

---

All you have to do to cheapen this life with sin is to do nothing. Stay as you are, and sin will kill you.

---

staying where they are. That's how it is with sin too. All you have to do to cheapen this life with sin is to do nothing. All you have to do to spend forever in hell instead of heaven is to do nothing. Stay as you are, and sin will kill you. God says, "Rid yourself of your sin." Get a new heart. And you can only do that at the cross, where Christ died for you, where He said, "Father, forgive them, for they do not know what they are doing" (Luke 23:34). He was forgiving you and me when He said that.

God has been warning you, knocking on the door, pursuing you, and He is saying, "If you stay where you are, you will die." Don't flirt with disaster. Move away from living your way. The storm is closer than it has ever been to your coast. Flee to the safety of the cross of Jesus Christ.

The Mission You Were Made For

Living As a
"Make a Difference" Person

Some of our great Hutchcraft family memories are of our camping vacations. Our son Doug knew that camping meant he was going to get his favorite breakfast of the year, Mom's Swedish pancakes. Those Swedish roll-ups are great stuff. Now, maybe you cook those at home, but we saved them for camping.

One beautiful morning in Vermont, Doug wasn't real anxious to wake up. I went back to the tent and said, "Doug, Swedish pancakes." One eye opened at that point, and he said, "Okay, I'll be out." A long time later, he finally staggered out of the tent. Unfortunately, there hadn't been any Swedish pancakes left for an hour. That trip was years ago, but to this day, Doug still remembers that morning. He recently told me, "You know what, Dad? I cannot believe I slept through the very thing I was hungry for." Let's take a God-moment about . . .

Sleeping through the Feast

Our word from the Word of God comes from Romans 13, beginning at verse 11. "Do this, understanding the present time. The hour has come for you to wake up from your slumber, because our salvation is nearer now than when we first believed. The night is nearly over; the day is almost here. So let us put aside the deeds of darkness and put on the armor of light." Paul says God's grand finale is approaching. It is closer than it has ever been. This is no time to be asleep, like a little camper who slept through all the good stuff. Too many Christians are sleeping through the most decisive days in the history of the church.

Everywhere I go, I find a deep spiritual restlessness in God's people. They don't know what it is for, but there is a deep sense that their Christian life is supposed to be more powerful. I have read the Book of Acts, heard about the power of Christians in other parts of the world, and I want the real thing.

THE MISSION YOU WERE MADE FOR

God's people are hungry. There is every indication that God is preparing a feast.

In these days some Christian leaders who have a window on God's work all over the country have said there is the greatest prayer movement growing they've ever seen. One leader said

---

> *Paul says God's grand finale is approaching. It is closer than it has ever been. This is no time to be asleep, like a little camper who slept through all the good stuff.*

---

that six of the seven signs that Charles Finney says precede great revivals are now present in our country. There is a general feeling that time is short. We have that great promise in Acts 2:17 that "in the last days, God says, I will pour out my Spirit on all people." Another Christian leader has said that he has never seen more open doors for the Gospel at one time in this century than he does now. The question is not whether Jesus is preparing a mighty work and a spiritual feast. It is whether you or I will be in on it—or whether we're going to sleep through it.

God has given the call for a feast that He is going to have, and too many of us are preoccupied with things that don't matter. This is no time to be coasting along on spiritual cruise control, business as usual, slacking off on the work of Jesus. The Second Coming Express is in high gear. Don't you hear it? This is a time for extraordinary prayer, for spiritual risk taking, for cleaning out the spiritual garbage that you've tolerated before, for asking the Lord, over and over again, to send a revival to your church, your neighborhood, your school. This is a time for expecting the supernatural and for attempting the supernatural. Go for God's gold in your life. God is preparing the powerful work that your restless heart is hungry for, so don't sleep through it.

lass reunions are interesting occasions. There are people you haven't seen for years, they haven't seen you. You go hoping you will recognize people and that they will recognize you. And you're bound to hear, "Hey, I remember you, but with hair. Didn't you used to have teeth? Didn't you used to have a body?" Frankly, conversations can be pretty superficial because you don't have much in common anymore, but once in awhile, you stop impressing each other enough to get into something important. That happened to a doctor friend of mine at his forty-fifth high school reunion. My doctor friend is a committed follower of Jesus Christ. He was catching up with a highly successful orthodontist who is a self-proclaimed atheist, but this orthodontist said to my doctor friend, "So talk to me about what you believe." My friend was pretty surprised to hear that from this particular fellow. Then this man gave his reason for asking. He said, "Frankly, I'm nervous about eternity." Let's take a God-moment about being . . .

Nervous about Eternity

Our word from the Word of God comes from Hebrews 9:27. It gives us a glimpse of the beginning of eternity for us. "Man is destined to die once, and after that to face judgment." You say, "That's what I was afraid of." The Bible confirms that we have an undeniable, uncancelable, unpostponable appointment with God for judgment. This orthodontist was refreshingly honest when he said, "I'm nervous about eternity." Most of us know that feeling. Sometimes we feel it when a friend, loved one, or coworker dies, and for a little while we think about eternity. I have had teenagers ask me at a funeral, "What if that was me?" Sometimes we think about eternity when we have had a close call or in those quiet moments when thoughts we usually try to bury come to center stage.

Actually, it is a good idea to be nervous about eternity. It's going to last a lot longer than these seventy years here that we think about constantly. People everywhere seem to know in their soul that there is something between them and God. Something's wrong there. We know there is a moral reckoning and moral bill to be paid for the sins of our lives. Wouldn't it be great to know that there was nothing to fear, that your eternity was secure?

Well, this might be the best news you have ever heard. Romans 5:8 says, "God demonstrates his own love for us in this: While we were still sinners [that means a wall between God and us because we've run our own lives], Christ died for us." Romans 8:1 says, "There is now no condemnation for those who are in Christ Jesus." See, sin is what will keep you out of heaven, but Jesus paid for that sin when He died on the cross. If you put your trust in Him and His death for you, you can trade in a death penalty for eternal life. John 5:24 says it beautifully. "I tell you the truth, whoever hears my word and believes him who sent me has eternal life and will not be condemned; he has crossed over from death to life."

The Plains Indians used to face the threat of prairie fires, so they burned a field between their village and the fire. They said, "The fire cannot go where the fire has already been." Why don't you go to the place where the fire for your sin fell on God's Son at the cross and claim His forgiveness? Dr. James Kennedy asks people, "If you died tonight, and God asked you, 'Why should I let you into My heaven?' what would you tell Him?" That's a good question. You could say the only right answer, "Lord, I have trusted in the work that Your only Son did on the cross." Once you have been to the cross, you don't ever have to be nervous about eternity again.

A city I visited missed the hurricane that hit the South, but we did get two days of the wet weather leftovers. We had drenching rain. Compared to the hurricane we had it easy, but the rain really soaked us. One morning while it was pouring, I drove by a bank and saw something that made me laugh. The sprinklers came on right on schedule. They were doing a beautiful job of watering the lawn, which really didn't need any more water. Let's take a God-moment about . . .

Soaking the Soaked

Our word from the Word of God comes from the Book of 2 Kings with a curious story in the seventh chapter. The capital city of Samaria is under siege, and the Syrian army has cut off all food. The city is starving to death. Conditions are desperate, with people resorting to cannibalism to stay alive. Now, there are four lepers who live outside the city, and they decide that since they are already going to die, they will surrender to the other army. They hope that maybe they will be taken as prisoners of war and be fed. When they get there, God has performed a miracle. The camp has been emptied out, so they find food and empty tents left there for them. They stuff themselves all night, then in verse 9, "They said to each other, 'We're not doing right. [It's about time they figured that out!] This is a day of good news and we are keeping it to ourselves. If we wait until daylight, punishment will overtake us. Let's go at once and report this.'" What a scene! These four men are sitting on this pile of food while multitudes are starving. A Christian from the former Soviet Union once said to a team my daughter was on, "The problem with American Christians is, you are overfeed." He's right. We are very blessed. We are soaked with blessings that no Christians have ever had before. We have Christian everything—radio, TV, rallies, conferences, trips, concerts, and seminars, but it's almost all for us. We are already stuffed, but we line up for another helping of blessing.

We are already soaked, but we turn on the sprinklers for more showers of blessing.

Something is wrong here. Let's not forget where our Master's heart is. He said, "I have come to seek and to save not that which is found, but that which is lost." He talks about a harvest where "the harvest is plentiful, but I can't find laborers to go get it." A self-focused church, a self-focused Christian, is not the will of God. We follow a Savior who left the safety of heaven, who lived among the lost, and who laid down His life to bring them home to God. He cannot be very happy with us when we focus on going to our Christian meetings, committees, and conferences; listening to our Christian speakers and songs; staying busy with our Christian schedules. Meanwhile, the spiritually destitute are starving to death, just like those people back in 2 Kings 7.

Like our Master, we need to live our lives for the lost people He gave His life for. Plenty of lives get no spiritual rain. Let's not aim our sprinklers at the already soaked. Let's take them to the places where it never rains.

o you look forward to seeing how you look in pictures? You say, "Well, uh . . . yes and no." There are always a *couple* of pictures you get back that you *would* like to look at again. You think, "Hey, I don't look too bad in that picture." But there are also always a couple you would like to throw away before anyone else sees them. If you're a photographer, or if you know the photographer, you don't have to wait to see how you look in the final photos. For example, we knew our photographer pretty well at our wedding, so he gave us our wedding pictures in contact prints. My wife is also a photographer, so I asked, "Honey, how do those contact prints work?" She said, "You place the negative right up against the photographic paper, you shine a light on it, and the image transfers directly to the paper." There you are, beautiful or ugly, as the case may be. Now, if there is even a little distance between the negative and the paper, you see a fuzzy or distorted image. You cannot transfer the image unless there is close contact. Let's take a God-moment about . . .

No Contact, No Transfer

Our word from the Word of God comes from Ezekiel 3, beginning with verse 11. "Go now to your countrymen in exile and speak to them. Say to them, 'This is what the Sovereign LORD says,' whether they listen or fail to listen." So Ezekiel goes and prepares himself for that. Verse 15 says, "I came to the exiles who lived at Tel Abib near the Kebar River. And there, where they were living, I sat among them for seven days—overwhelmed."

Ezekiel was just like us. He had a message to deliver, which was just a little different from ours, since we speak about a cross where Christ died. Ezekiel says the way he prepared himself was to sit in the middle of the exiles, get in touch with them, and allow his heart to be overwhelmed with what was happening to them. You cannot reach others if you don't know them.

Much research shows that the first year after people become Christians, they know a lot of lost people from their old life. Five years into their Christian lives, they have virtually no non-

> *The image will not transfer if there is no close contact. Evangelism is just a religious concept unless you are close to some lost people, transferring to them the image of Christ.*

Christian friends. All the salt is in the saltshaker, all the light is blazing together in one corner, while most of the world is totally dark. We disappear into Christianhood. We lose all our meaningful contact with people who have not heard.

What non-Christian are you meaningfully close to? It is like that contact print. The image will not transfer if there is no close contact. Evangelism is just a religious concept unless you are close to some lost people, transferring to them the image of Christ. Do you know your neighbors? Do you take some time to get into the lives of your coworkers, or do you just pass by them? Ask God to lay some of those people, by name, on your heart. Build some bridges to them. Find ways to show them you care. Take the risk of reaching out, and if you have to stay home from church to have them over for dinner, then do it.

"We will have all eternity to celebrate our victories, but only a few short hours to win them," said the great missionary Amy Carmichael. If we are too busy doing things for Jesus so that we don't have time to get close to the people He died for, then we are too busy. You have a Savior, you have a heaven, you have eternal life to transfer, and you can't do it unless there is close contact. You cannot reach them if you don't touch them.

Our daughter and son-in-law have a big red van. This van has two seats in the front and a bench seat in the back, and in between there's nothing but carpeted open floor. Now, it is always challenging to talk in there, and it is almost impossible when the windows are open. One hot day we were all zipping along the interstate with the wind roaring around us, trying to communicate from back to front and front to back. My wife happened to be driving, and I could see her lips moving. I had no idea what she was saying. I tried to talk to her and the same thing happened. She knew I was saying something, but she had no idea what it was. See, in that van, it doesn't matter how loud you talk, how sincere you are, or how important your words are. They cannot hear what you are saying. Let's take a God-moment about . . .

Getting Through

Our word from the Word of God comes from Matthew 13. Jesus says, "A farmer went out to sow his seed. As he was scattering the seed, some fell along the path, and the birds came and ate it up" (v. 4). That seed never stood a chance. In verse 19 Jesus explains that "when anyone hears the message about the kingdom and does not understand it, the evil one comes and snatches away what was sown in his heart." This is hard ground when the Gospel is heard. There's no response. I used to think this was someone who just wasn't interested in the good news about Jesus, but this doesn't say they didn't want the Gospel. It doesn't say they rejected the Gospel. It says they didn't understand it.

There have never been as many Christians who have as much Christianity as we do. We have Christian everything, but we are surrounded by post-Christian neighbors, friends, and coworkers who don't know there's a right or wrong, don't know there's a Gospel, don't ever plan to go to a religious meeting to hear a religious speaker talk on a religious subject, and who don't understand our meetings or our language. Why are we so disconnected from each other? It's easy to say, "Oh, they're rejecting the Lord." Are they rejecting the Lord, or are they rejecting our Christian language? They don't know what our words mean. It's like a mission field where the missionaries speak in their own language instead of the language of the native. They don't understand the word *sin* anymore, or *believe* or *born again* or *accept Christ* or *personal Savior* or any number of words. It's like the scene in our wind-whipped van. They see our lips moving, but they haven't a clue as to what we are saying. It doesn't matter how loudly we present the Gospel, how sincere we are, or how life or death the information is. They just can't figure out what we're trying to say.

Since we do have a life-or-death message, and since we have a life-or-death responsibility to get it out, we have to translate the message—not just transmit it. To translate the Gospel means to put it into their words and go the extra mile to communicate it so they will understand. I think we have three challenges. Number one, love those lost people in their language and be in the places that matter to them. Also, find needs they have in their lives and help meet those needs so they know you love them in Christ. Second, live for Christ in their language. Be a better employee because you are a Christian. Be a better employer, be a better neighbor, son, daughter, mom, dad, whatever. Do the things that will show them the difference Christ makes in a way that will matter to them. Third, speak the Gospel in their language. Since relationships are so important, talk about the Gospel as life's most important relationship. This is a relationship you're *supposed* to have, you *don't* have because of sin, you *can* have because of Jesus, and one you *must* choose. Make sure you translate the Gospel. Don't just shout it across the bridge to lost people. Many who desperately need Jesus are at the other end, unable to understand. It's too important for us to not get through. Will you move across that gap?

I love to spend a couple of days in Ocean City, New Jersey, right along the Atlantic Coast. Maybe it's because I grew up in the middle of the country, where I never knew what an ocean was. We like to rent bikes, riding the long boardwalk there at Ocean City very early in the morning when hardly anybody else is around. At one end is this white building with the initials O.C.B.P., which stands for Ocean City Beach Patrol. Occasionally, you'll see the lifeguards meeting there early in the morning, discussing their day's assignments. You won't see them meeting there in the afternoon. If you're at the beach, you don't want them meeting in their little building in the afternoon. Mr. Lifeguard is up where he's supposed to be, in his high chair, and he's focused on the people in the water. That's how one of them, several years ago when I was there, spotted three children who were in trouble—perhaps about to drown. He cleared the beach, got the other lifeguards, plunged in and saved those kids. It's a good thing they weren't having a lifeguard meeting up on the boardwalk. Let's take a God-moment about . . .

When Lifeguards Forget the Beach

Our word from the Word of God is John 10:15–16. Jesus said, "I lay down my life for the sheep. I have other sheep that are not of this sheep pen. I must bring them also."

Not long ago, I had the privilege of being in Westminster Abbey in London, where for over a thousand years they have buried some of the greatest people of British history. Many of the kings and queens of all those centuries are buried there, some literary and music greats, and one missionary. His tomb is in a central spot and is one of the first you see. David Livingstone. The great man who introduced the Gospel of Jesus to much of Africa. He sacrificed the comforts of England to go and bury his life there. He sensitized his country to the needs of Africa, in what was then known as darkest Africa. He is considered one of England's greatest men. I stood over that vault in the floor there and read the facts about his life, then noticed the verses from John 10.

It really moved me, reading those verses on David Livingstone's tomb. Other sheep I must bring. I can't be content with the ones already in the fold. Livingstone devoted his life to the sheep who weren't in the fold yet. So did Jesus. Have you? You

---

See, we who know Christ are God's lifeguards. We are assigned to rescue other dying people as we were rescued.

---

don't necessarily have to go to Africa or to any foreign mission field. You are surrounded at work, in school, and in your neighborhood by sheep who aren't in yet. They don't know Jesus the Shepherd who said, "I lay down my life for the sheep."

See, we who know Christ are God's lifeguards. We are assigned to rescue other dying people as we were rescued. The problem is, we tend to get in our lifeguard station—church—and stay there. We have lifeguard meetings, lifeguard songs, we take lifeguard offerings, and we have lifeguard equipment, but we forget to go to the beach where the people who need us are. When is the last time you left the safety of the comfortable lifeguard station and plunged into the surf to bring Jesus to someone? We can't settle for not having any unbelieving friends and simply saying, "Well, all my friends are Christians." No, not until we get to heaven. We can't settle for just feeding ourselves in the lifeguard station while people are drowning in the surf.

Our Lord's magnificent obsession was people who weren't in yet. Will you let Him put that passion in your heart? Get strong in the lifeguard meetings, but don't stay in the meetings. You're needed at the beach.

Someday I might be banned from restaurants. I have been known to give the help a hard time. Now, that is not really what I'm trying to do. I figure that waiting on people sometimes gets humdrum and boring, and too often customers treat you like part of the menu or a vending machine. So I think it's fun to inject some laughs into their day. For example, I have been known to walk into a restaurant, and the lady will ask, "Table for two?" I'll say, "Well, yes, but we have a busload of about thirty-eight junior high students waiting. Should we bring them in now?" There's a priceless look on her face. I immediately let her know that I am kidding. I always ask for the server's name by telling him or her that "my mother told me to never talk to strangers." And when ordering one of my favorite sandwiches, I have been known to ask, "Is Patty in?" "Patty who?" the waitress innocently asks. "Patty Melt," I reply, and her eyes disappear to the top of her head.

I just try to lighten up their lives. We also try to encourage and really compliment them. Sometimes I will tell the server, "Hey, you are a great cook." They look a little unsure about how to react to that. They will say, "Oh, I didn't cook it. I just serve it." I knew that. Let's take a God-moment about . . .

The Power Preposition

Our word from the Word of God comes from 1 Corinthians 3:5. Here is what Paul says about himself and another great Christian leader of that time, Apollos. "What, after all, is Apollos? And what is Paul? Only servants, through whom you came to believe—as the Lord has assigned to each his task." I am sure there were people who would have said, "Paul got me to Christ. Apollos got me to Christ." But Paul said, "No, I didn't. It wasn't from me. It was *through* me." There is the power preposition. We are only servants *through* whom, not *by* whom, not *from* whom, only *through* whom others come to believe.

Now, it is like a server in a restaurant. It is not her recipe or her effort. She just delivers what someone else has worked on and made possible. That is what Jesus was saying when He said, "I am the vine; you are the branches" (John 15:5). The branch doesn't produce the fruit. It looks like it is producing the fruit, but it comes from the vine, *through* the branches.

Do you know what this means to you? You can risk doing for the Lord certain things you thought were too much for you. You can dare to open your mouth about Jesus. You can dare to step up to that leadership role. You can dare to start that Christian group, prayer fellowship, or Bible study. You can dare to say yes to an assignment from the Lord that you have been saying no to. Why? Because the Bible says in 1 Thessalonians 5:24, "The one who calls you is faithful and he will do it." Philippians 2:13 says, "It is God who works in you to will and to act according to his good purpose." God will give you the words and God will give you the insight. God will give you the plan, and He will give you the methods and the strength. Any true work for Christ is Christ doing the work *through* you, not you doing the work for Him. *Through* is the preposition that opens up your life to all kinds of powerful new possibilities. So just be available. There are many meals I would have never eaten in a restaurant if it had been up to the waiter or waitress to grow and prepare the food, but they were able to deliver it. That is what Paul says we are, only servants. That is what your Lord is asking you to be, someone to deliver to hungry lives what He has prepared for them. Now, you could serve it, couldn't you?

American television viewers know more about how the police operate then we ever needed to know. Real-life shows that portray actual days in the lives of policemen, government agents, or various other law enforcers are all the rave today. We've ridden in squad cars, heard all the conversations, seen them make arrests. And after awhile, we start to pick up some police vocabulary. For example, a car is dispatched to the scene of a crime, and the officer finds out that it's not something that one officer can handle or should tackle alone, so he or she shouts this one important word into his radio mike: "Backup. I need backup." Immediately, more officers are dispatched to the scene to back him up; and that teamwork, that reinforcement, can make the difference. Let's take a God-moment about . . .

Going In with Backup

Our word from the Word of God comes from Ephesians 6:18–20. The apostle Paul is calling for backup. "And pray in the Spirit on all occasions, with all kinds of prayers and requests. With this in mind, be alert and always keep on praying for all the saints. Pray also for me, that whenever I open my mouth, words may be given me so that I will fearlessly make known the mystery of the gospel, for which I am an ambassador in chains. Pray that I may declare it fearlessly, as I should." Basically, Paul tells his backup people, "What happens when I preach depends on what happens when you pray." Paul's going in on his mission, but he can't go in without backup. Right now, there is someone who needs you to be doing that same thing for them.

Not long ago, I was on an airplane flight from Chicago to Newark, and I got into a conversation with the woman next to me that led into the subject of relationships. I told her that I talk about relationships for a living—and especially life's most important relationship. She said, "What's that?" I was glad she asked, and I had a great opportunity to explain in depth to her why we need a Savior and how she could know Christ. She said, "Do you have a card?" She wanted to know more. She wanted to know how to talk to her husband about it, who's from a totally different background. She was so open to Christ, so I sent her additional information. She was *very* open to hear about Jesus. As I was collecting my baggage after the flight, somebody called my name, and a man I recognized introduced himself to me. I said, "Lee, what have you been doing?" He said, "I've been praying for you." I said, "Boy, that's great. What do you mean?" He said, "I've been three rows behind you on the plane, and when I saw that you were talking to that lady, I prayed that you would have an opportunity to speak to her about Christ and that she'd be really open." So that's why her heart was so open! I said, "Lee, do you know what the police call this? Backup."

Well, who are you backing up, and who is *your* backup? There's an invisible but decisive connection between one person's prayer and the other person's result. You don't usually get to see it as I did after that flight, but it's always there. Sometimes I have struggled before I've had to preach in important meetings, and I've said, "Lord, those people who said they're praying for me, get them praying now. It's an hour before I speak, and I can't get it together." And it has come together. Those people must have been praying. Ask the Lord for promptings to pray for people. Listen to those promptings, obey them, and commit yourself to your pastor, teacher, a spiritual leader, or a missionary and say, "I'm going to be their backup." When you do, you're participating in the war for this world in ways you can't see, but it may make all the difference. Be backup for the members of your family. Frequently intercede for them, wherever they are today, and ask the Lord to give you some brothers and sisters who will back you up. Don't go out there alone. What a way for your life to count more. One of God's servants is out there calling headquarters right now, pleading, "Send me backup," and through the miracle of prayer, God will send you.

Ellis Island was the first piece of America that millions of immigrants ever touched. It is a little island in the shadow of the Statue of Liberty in New York Harbor. When you visit the island, you see a long, granite wall with thousands of names of immigrants who passed through there. This was the point of entry for all the immigrants coming through New York. They would book passage and get the cheapest price they could, way down below the decks. Finally, the boat would reach America, they would step off, and they would enter this long, red brick building on Ellis Island. It's cavernous and echoes on the inside. They had to go through certain steps that eventually permitted them to move from the island and on to their real destination, which was New York City and the mainland. The tour guide said the people carried all their belongings in a basket. Well, that was okay. They knew the island was not where they would live, so out of all those thousands who came, not one ever set up a house there. They were not going to be there very long. Let's take a God-moment about . . .

A Basketful of Earth

Our word from the Word of God comes from 1 Peter 1, beginning at verse 1. Peter writes to "God's elect, strangers in the world." Remembering that image of believers, go on to verse 17. He says, "Live your lives as strangers here in reverent fear." In 2:11 he continues, "Dear friends, I urge you as aliens and strangers in the world, to abstain from sinful desires." Peter says, "This isn't home." It's like the old hymn, "This world is not my home, I'm just passing through. My treasures are laid up somewhere beyond the blue."

We are all immigrants, according to the Bible. Earth is our Ellis Island. We have seventy years here that are just the preparation for billions of years, but the quality of the billions of years is determined by how we live the seventy. Here is a question: If we are just immigrants passing through earth, why are we setting up so much stuff here on Ellis Island? In Luke 12

Jesus addresses this issue of accumulation. He says in verse 22, "Do not worry about your life, what you will eat; or about your body, what you will wear." He says some radical stuff in verse 24. "Consider the ravens: They do not sow or reap, they have no storeroom or barn; yet God feeds them. And how

---

We are all immigrants, according to the Bible. Earth is our Ellis Island.

---

much more valuable you are than birds!" He is saying that for our security, we don't need a stored-up reserve somewhere. That is the opposite of everything we have been taught about security. But here is biblical security. Jesus continues, "Your Father knows that you need [these things]. . . . Sell your possessions and give to the poor. Provide purses for yourselves that will not wear out, a treasure in heaven that will not be exhausted, where no thief comes near and no moth destroys. For where your treasure is, there your heart will be also" (vv. 30, 33–34). There's no storeroom, no pile of earth stuff. Send it ahead to the place where you are going to live. Don't accumulate it in the place you are just visiting.

We are all guilty of the sin of accumulating. We build that earth kingdom, earth reserves, and earth security. One day Jesus may come back and say, "What are you doing with all that tied up? I had a world to reach." He calls us to live simply on this immigrant island and to pour everything else into eternal causes. Give that for which He gave everything He had. If you want a bankful of heaven, then be content with a basketful of earth.

A little known episode of American history came to light in the movie *Glory* a few years ago. The Academy Award–winning film called attention to some unsung heroes from the Civil War—heroes no matter which side, blue or gray, you might favor. They were the 54th regiment of Massachusetts, under the command of Colonel Robert Shaw. What was unusual about them was this: The entire company of men was black except for Colonel Shaw, and they left behind a tremendous example of courage. There is an extremely intense scene in the movie when Colonel Shaw learns that President Lincoln wants a recent Confederate States of America resolution read to them. It has just been passed by the Confederates, and it says that all Negro soldiers will be summarily executed if they are taken prisoner. Any soldier in their command and anyone commanding them will also be put to death. It is night as that entire company stands in the pouring rain and soberly listens to that being read. Shaw finally retires to his tent having told his men that he would be happy to sign the discharge papers of anyone who wants to leave the next morning. As he goes to bed, he doesn't even know if he will have an army in the morning. Well, he did. Let's take a God-moment about how . . .

The Price Is Right

When Colonel Shaw rose the next morning, he found his entire company was still there. Not one man had left, and later they attempted to take a Confederate fort near Charleston. President Lincoln called their heroism "one of the turning points of the Civil War," because 180,000 black troops signed up to fight after that battle at the Charleston fort. This is an example of men who saw a turning point in their lives—the cost was spelled out to them, they counted the cost, and they made the commitment.

Our word from the Word of God comes from Luke 9, beginning at verse 57. "As they were walking along the road, a man said to [Jesus], 'I will follow you wherever you go.' Jesus replied,

'Foxes have holes and birds of the air have nests, but the Son of Man has no place to lay his head.' He said to another man, 'Follow me.' But the man replied, 'Lord, first let me go and bury my father.'" His father probably hadn't died, it was perhaps just a matter of, "I want to stay home a little longer." Jesus said to him, "Let the dead bury their own dead, but you go

---

> ### *Basically, Jesus is saying, "If you follow Me, I'm going to give you the price tag. It will cost you comfort, personal plans, and rights that others may want to hang on to."*

---

and proclaim the kingdom of God." Finally, Jesus says, "No one who puts his hand to the plow and looks back is fit for service in the kingdom of God."

Basically, Jesus is saying, "If you follow Me, I'm going to give you the price tag. It will cost you comfort, personal plans, and rights that others may want to hang on to. It may reorder some relationships." The difference between Jesus and Satan is that Satan does not tell you what something is going to cost. Jesus tells you in advance. Going your own way will cost you deeply. Jesus will tell you that. Satan won't.

We distort the Gospel when we try to discount it. Jesus calls us to a lifestyle that says, "All other agendas will take second place to Yours, Lord. I understand You paid a high price for me, and I am willing to pay one for You." The bigger the thing you are living for, the more important your life will be—and there is nothing bigger than living for Christ. He is the One you were created for, and He is looking for heroes who won't say, "I will, but first . . ." Just, "I will." Yes, it costs a lot to follow Christ. But it costs more not to—a wasted life. In a war long ago, some soldiers knew it could cost them everything, yet they made their commitment. In the war for people's lives, Jesus says, "I have paid the price. Will you?" You have probably sung this song, now I hope you will live it: "I have decided to follow Jesus. No turning back."

have many memories from the times our team ministered on the Navajo reservation in Arizona and New Mexico. We're always busy with evangelism, but we did have one day off. So we all packed into a van to go see this spectacular canyon. It was approaching dark as we were returning, and we thought, "There are two ways back, and we have to get up early tomorrow morning for a meeting." One way was long but paved, and the other was short but unpaved across the mountain. We decided we would take the short road, even though it was a little bumpy. I started driving, then Karen took over, and all of a sudden we felt the van lurching, and she said, "Oh, no. I think we're out of gas. I can't believe it." Someone had mentioned briefly that there was a problem with the fuel gauge before we left, so I glanced at it before we left town, and it said three quarters of a tank. Now, it would have been a good idea to fill up before we left civilization, and since we didn't, here we sat in the dark on a lonely back road forty miles from the nearest town, praying like crazy. Thank God, He sent us a Good Samaritan who went forty miles for gas. So Ron, did you learn anything? Let's take a God-moment about . . .

Leaving without a Fill-Up

Our word from the Word of God comes from Luke 24, beginning at verse 47. God is preparing His people to do a job for Him. Here is what Jesus said to His disciples. "Repentance and forgiveness of sins will be preached in his name to all nations, beginning at Jerusalem. You are witnesses of these things. I am going to send you what my Father has promised; but stay in the city until you have been clothed with power from on high."

God has great things in store for us, and great things He would like to accomplish through our lives. Imagine the disciples saying, "Well, let's get to work." They're ready to run out the door and start doing, but He says, "Wait, stay. Wait for the power first." Maybe that is why many of us have flopped when we try to do something for the Lord. We ran off to do it before we got the power to do it, just like when I set off on that trip without filling up with fuel and ended up stranded. Maybe you have had days like that spiritually, or while trying to work for the Lord. Maybe you have started off your day but were in too big a hurry to be with the Lord for very long. You didn't wait for His power. There was probably so much to do, but you ran out of gas right in the middle. It didn't work. Again, you didn't do what Jesus says here. "Stay, and wait until you have been clothed with power from on high."

Jesus said, "Stay and wait until you have been clothed with power from on high." Don't run out in your spiritual unmentionables to live for the Lord or to serve Him.

Jesus likened it to getting dressed. He said, "Don't go out unclothed." Don't run out in your spiritual unmentionables to live for the Lord or to serve Him. We have to take time to get prayed up before we start running for Jesus. The prayer meeting needs to precede any other meeting. We have to be in His Book, looking for His personal guidance. We have to get on our knees or face and resurrender to Him for that day or that work. We need to come to a point of seeing that we are unworthy and powerless when it comes to doing anything for Jesus and then let His power take us over.

My reservation drive wasn't the first trip where I left without a fill-up. I have done that spiritually too many times. Maybe you have too. Right now, slow down, and pull over to God's great fuel tank. You're not going to finish your journey if you don't take time to fill up before you go.

have spent only a few days in Israel, and they were unforgettable. But sometimes they were disillusioning. I went to the basement of a church along the Via Dolorosa, and I will never forget that basement because this was where Jesus was tried before Pilate. There are still large cobblestones there in the basement in an area the New Testament calls the "Stone Pavement." This is where Jesus was hauled before that mob and where the soldiers stripped Him and taunted Him. Here they played "The Game of the King," where they selected one prisoner a week to humiliate and mock just for their own entertainment. After the walking tour moved on, I stayed behind in that place and had a silent moment, realizing I was standing where my Lord had been humiliated for me. I walked up the stairs, still dwelling on that sacrifice, and as I walked out into the sunlight, I was greeted by a garish orange and yellow sign on a booth right in front of the stairs. It said, "Christ's Suffering Souvenirs." Let's take a God-moment about . . .

None of Your Business

Our word from the Word of God comes from Luke 9, beginning at verse 2. Jesus is giving His marching orders to His disciples. "And he sent them out to preach the kingdom of God and to heal the sick. He told them: 'Take nothing for the journey—no staff, no bag, no bread, no money, no extra tunic. Whatever house you enter, stay there until you leave that town. If people do not welcome you, shake the dust off your feet when you leave their town, as a testimony against them.' So they set out and went from village to village, preaching the gospel and healing people everywhere."

This really represents the roots of all ministry for Jesus. Did you notice, His ministry is simple, uncomplicated, unconcerned about money, unencumbered. His people travel light. When I traveled to Haiti, I talked to a Haitian believer who had come to the United States and been in a church for a short time. He said, "You know what I noticed in America? It seems like Christianity is a business." That really bothered me because anywhere and anytime Christianity becomes a business, it has left the model of Jesus. I once heard about a young Christian who visited a large Christian convention with a friend of mine. He toured the exposition floor, with all of its marketing, products, and religious wares. When he went outside for a breather, he said to my friend, "And just think, all of this started at Calvary."

I was disgusted when I saw that sign about the souvenirs in Israel, commercializing the pure, redemptive work of Christ. But unfortunately, that travesty is not limited to a few souvenir shops in the Holy Land. When we follow the money instead of the mission, we have let the faith work of God's kingdom become a business. When our mission and personal obedience decisions are based on a financial bottom line or a profit and loss statement, we have lost our way. While God's work should be done in a businesslike way, it should never become a business or ruled by business values. For example, try to find a five-year plan in the New Testament. You won't, because Jesus and His followers were spontaneous there. It is not necessarily bad to have a plan, as long as we stay Spirit-spontaneous and don't become *controlled* by a plan. Many Spirit-directed choices don't add up with earth math but only with the miracle math of Jesus used by men and women of faith.

On your list of business things to be done, make sure the work of Jesus Christ is none of your business. It is too big. It is too bold. It is too uncomplicated. It is too full of God's surprises to be contained in a business box. The life and death of Jesus, so freely given, are just too precious and pure to become a vehicle for personal advancement and gain. Remember, the only time Jesus ever carried a whip was when He found money changers in the house of God.

Nancy got off to a fast start spiritually—in a way. It took two years of coming to my Campus Life club before she finally chose Christ as her Savior, but after that she really took off. Not long after she made her commitment, she came over to our house with a problem. Nancy had come home talking about Jesus, and her big sister Linda said, "Sure, Nancy. Last week it was a drug, next week it will be a boyfriend, this week it's Jesus. You'll get over it." Nancy said to me, "I need to know how to convince Linda. Can you give me an argument to make her know this is real?" I said, "Well, maybe I could, but I'd rather you do this, Nancy. Ask yourself this question: What change could I ask Jesus to make in me that my big sister Linda would have to notice?" She said, "I got it." Two weeks later Nancy came back. I said, "How's it going with the Lord and with Linda?" She said, "Oh, great. I gave God the chair." I said, "You what?" She said, "I gave God the chair. See, we have this big, red, overstuffed chair in our living room. It's right by the picture window, right in front of the TV set, and Linda and I always argue over who's going to get it. I just said, 'Lord, help me to be unselfish about this chair.'" Wouldn't you know that really began to get Linda's attention. She said, "Nancy, what's happened to you?"

Two years later, big sister Linda came to me and said, "Ron, Nancy and I just wanted you to know that I've just given my life to Christ." I said, "Terrific." She said, "Yeah, but we have a question. Who gets the chair?" That really happened! Let's take a God-moment about . . .

Undeniable Evidence

Our word from the Word of God comes from Matthew 5:15–16. "Neither do people light a lamp and put it under a bowl. Instead they put it on its stand, and it gives light to everyone in the house. In the same way, let your light shine before men, that they may see your good deeds and praise your Father in heaven." Notice it doesn't say that they will hear your good beliefs and praise your Father in heaven. They will see your good deeds. Look at 1 Peter 2:12; it's like a companion verse. "Live such good lives among the pagans that, though they accuse you of doing wrong, they may see your good deeds and glorify God on the day he visits us."

People who start out criticizing you end up praising your God. Why? Well, it's not beliefs or meetings that interest people in your Jesus. It's a changed life. It's those good deeds. Maybe you need to ask yourself, in light of the lost people in your world, "What change could I ask Jesus to make in me that they would have to notice?" If you are concerned for a parent who

---

Maybe you need to ask yourself, in light of the lost people in your world, "What change could I ask Jesus to make in me that they would have to notice?"

---

doesn't know the Lord, ask yourself, "How could I give them a better son or daughter? With me being a Christian, my parent should get a better son or daughter out of me. More time with them, more help around the house, more respect, more honoring them should come from me." Make changes they would have to notice. Maybe you're a parent, and you have a son or daughter who doesn't know the Lord. Ask yourself, "What change could I have Jesus make in me, as a mom or dad, that they would really notice?" Who can be against something that gives them a better parent or a better child? Maybe you're an employee and you want to reach your employer. You say, "Lord, how could I change? Make me more reliable, more on time, more conscientious, whatever they would have to notice."

Be a better friend or a better neighbor. Be different in the way that would matter most to the lost person you want to reach for Christ. For Nancy, it was that chair in the living room. Give the people around you a new and improved you, daily made possible by Jesus Christ. It will win you the right to introduce them to the One who has changed you. They can't see Jesus, but they're looking at you, so show them in living color the life-changing power of Jesus Christ. A change that *matters* to them is undeniable evidence.

At certain times of the year, our lawn grows like the set of a Tarzan movie. One time after we had been gone for two or three weeks, we came home to see the lawn taking over our neighborhood. Now, my son had been very, very busy during the summer, but he was finally available on this day when it was desperately needed. I said, "Okay, the lawn's high, but Brad and the mower are outside, ready to go." I was waiting for the beautiful music of that mower running. Nothing. Why? Brad came in and said, "Dad, I tried everything. The mower isn't working." Oh, this was frustrating. There's the need, here's the worker. Where's the tool? Let's take a God-moment about . . .

"Where's the Bullets?"

In David Schmitt's book *The Great Commission: Cause or Casualty?* the subtitle is *Perspective on the North American Churches' Stalled Commitment to World Evangelism*. He cites disturbing trends that I have seen too. "Christian magazine publishers say articles on missions and world evangelization are the least read in their publications. It is taking career missionaries longer each year to raise their support, or in other words, finding enough people to give. Denominations have missionary candidates ready to go, but no funds to send them." It's like Brad with the lawn mower. There's the need, there's the worker, but no tool to do it with—the money's not there. "Research shows that Baby Boomers are skipping missions oriented meetings at church. A growing portion of annual church budgets is being spent by local missionaries inside the church. Traditionally good giving churches have had to reduce their missions giving commitments." This has got to be heartbreaking to a God who sacrificed His one and only Son for this world. What's happening?

Our word from the Word of God comes from Haggai 1:5. The Lord Almighty says, "Give careful thought to your ways. You have planted much, but have harvested little. You eat, but never have enough. You drink, but never have your fill. You put on clothes, but are not warm. You earn wages, only to put them in a purse with holes in it." He is talking here about people who are successful but restless. Verses 7–9: "This is what the LORD Almighty says: 'Give careful thought to your ways.'" Now He's referring to the need to build His temple. "'Go up into the mountains and bring down timber and build the house, so that I may take pleasure in it and be honored,' says the LORD. 'You expected much, but see, it turned out to be little. What you brought home, I blew away. Why?' declares the LORD Almighty. 'Because of my house, which remains a ruin, while each of you is busy with his own house.'" Listen to those words. Busy with your own house. Could it be that we've been putting our best into our kingdom and leaving Him with the leftovers?

I remember a couple in their early twenties saying, "Our grandparents rearranged their whole lives around the work of reaching the world." Well, so did God. What about you? A friend who was giving a substantial gift to the Lord's work said, "Ron, I have to give this." He said, "What would happen if God had a soldier at the front line, there's the enemy, and this soldier's got his gun. He's trained. He's ready to fight, and suddenly he says, 'Hey, where's the bullets? They didn't give me any bullets.'" Well, today that's what is happening to the work of God. It's like the day we needed something to mow the lawn. We had a need, we had a worker, but not the equipment to do the job.

I remember a couple in their early twenties saying, "Our grandparents rearranged their whole lives around the work of reaching the world." Well, so did God. What about you?

In many places today, the work of God is standing paralyzed or limited because somebody isn't sending the bullets. We could be in the final battles for people's lives before Christ comes back, and you have been trusted with some of God's ammunition. That's not for you to sit on, to build your own house. This is no time for men and women on the front lines to be without bullets. Make this your battle. God's battles will be your battles. Commit to see that front-line soldiers have the ammunition they need.

Here is a little trivia quiz. What do these people have in common? James Haggerty, George Reedy, James Brady, and Marlin Fitzwater. Do you know what they are famous for? You have probably heard of at least one of them. They were all presidential press secretaries. Those are names you would have never heard of except for their connection to the president of the United States. When these relatively unknown people call a press conference, the Washington press corps starts to scramble, and they arrive in minutes. The press hang on every word these men speak, write them down, and then run to the phone to report it. Why do people consider the words these men speak so important? Well, because those are not their words. Let's take a God-moment about . . .

Words from Higher Up

Our word from the Word of God comes from 2 Corinthians 5:20. Paul says, "We are therefore Christ's ambassadors, as though God were making his appeal through us. We implore you on Christ's behalf: Be reconciled to God." This is an interesting role—you are an ambassador. If you know Christ, you are His ambassador. Now, an ambassador drops in on the prime minister of a country to which he is sent. He delivers a message, but it is not from him, it's from the president.

A common word in the New Testament describes proclaiming the good news about Jesus. It is usually rendered as *preach* in your English Bible. It literally means to deliver a message as a herald. What's a herald? In Bible times, a herald was the king's messenger, a kind of press secretary. He would ride into a village, open up his scroll, and everybody would gather around as he boldly made an announcement. Why was he so bold? He was not delivering a message from himself, so he wasn't afraid of what people might say. He was delivering a message from the king. So are you. Paul says, "On Christ's behalf." I am in Jesus' place. I need to say to my neighbor, my friend, my family member what He would say if He were here.

He would start by saying, "Get the wall down between you and God. Be reconciled to Him. Begin a relationship with Him through My work on the cross."

The modern equivalent of the herald would be the press secretary, and the principle is the same. You can speak with authority when you are delivering words from higher up. We seem to forget that when we are with people who don't know our Jesus. Often, they will intimidate us into silence. I cannot imagine the presidential press secretary looking at all those reporters and saying, "I'm scared. I have nothing to say to you." Imagine a herald freezing around people to whom he is supposed to deliver the king's message.

When it comes to us sharing our King's message, it is a life-and-death matter. A person will simply live and die and spend forever without God unless you bring Jesus to them. As you share, remember this isn't a matter of you trying to sign them up for your beliefs or for your church or to convince them to see it your way. Your mission is simply to deliver your King's message. Of course, be gentle and loving, not pushy. Build a relationship with them, but don't be timid, apologetic, or defensive.

The King has a message for the people around you, and He has entrusted it to you to deliver. He will even help you know how to say it as you share it. Deliver your life-saving news with all the authority of someone who has words that are from higher up.

A few years ago, the president of the United States came to speak in a town near us. Now, that's a rare opportunity, so I wanted our kids to see and hear a living president. We got there two hours early. There was a mass of people, it was hard to park, and we stood for two hours. Then the president was late. Finally, you could hear a ripple go through the crowd as they hung the presidential seal on the podium. "Ladies and gentlemen, the president of the United States." And there he was. It was worth the wait. Well, everybody gave him a great ovation that lasted quite awhile, and when the applause died down, he started to speak. While he spoke, nobody left. Of course not. When you come to hear someone important, you don't just applaud and leave. You stay after the applause to hear what he has to say. Let's take a God-moment about . . .

Dead-End Applause

Our word from the Word of God comes from Isaiah 6, perhaps the greatest worship scene in the Bible. The prophet Isaiah says in verse 1, "I saw the Lord seated on a throne, high and exalted, and the train of his robe filled the temple." Then he sees angelic beings who were calling to one another, "Holy, holy, holy is the LORD Almighty; the whole earth is full of his glory." Then Isaiah says, "At the sound of their voices the doorposts and thresholds shook and the temple was filled with smoke." Now, this is worship. This is praise, getting lost in the Lord, overwhelmed by the Lord. There's a wonderful new emphasis in many places today on praise and worship. It really brings the Lord close. It makes the Lord the focus when it's so easy to forget Him. We finally take time to forget ourselves and experience just how big God is.

That's sort of our standing ovation for God. Unfortunately, too many of us leave after the standing ovation, not realizing that's only the beginning. You see, God wants to speak. He wants to say some things to us. Look at verse 5. "'Woe to me!' I cried. 'I am ruined! For I am a man of unclean lips, and I live

246

among a people of unclean lips, and my eyes have seen the King, the LORD Almighty.'" You see, worship is supposed to lead to repentance. He says, "Wait a minute, when I see the Lord, I see His holiness, and I see the sin that I've not dealt with." You have to make things right with this awesome God. Worship that doesn't lead to cleaning up your sin is just dead-end applause.

Can we leave now? Well, no, because God hasn't even spoken yet. Verse 8 says, "Then I heard the voice of the Lord saying, 'Whom shall I send? And who will go for us?' And I said, 'Here am I. Send me!'" I see my sin, I get God's forgiveness, and then I suddenly see the people who don't have a Savior yet. My heart aches for those who haven't seen the King. See, worship is not just getting a good feeling because I got close to God. I see the Lord, and that makes me see the lost people who haven't gotten close to Him. Worship that is really worship will lead to repentance and then to evangelism.

"Here am I, Lord. I will go for You into the lives of the people around me who have yet to see the King as I have." You don't just go to God's presence to applaud, though that's a great place to start. You go to hear Him speak and then to act on what He says.

God has assigned me to two basic geographies in my life—metropolitan Chicago and metropolitan New York City—so my view of the night sky has been somewhat deprived. With haze and lots of bright lights, you cannot clearly see what is out there in the sky. Well, that wasn't a problem on my last trip to South Africa. While out in the highlands outside of Johannesburg, I could hear birds and sounds that were not part of my world back home, and the night was as dark as dark can be. On my last night there, after God had moved mightily in that conference, I took a walk and was thinking about Him and talking to Him. As I looked up at the sky, I saw a constellation called the Southern Cross. It is a small cluster of stars that form a cross in the sky over that hemisphere. You cannot see these stars where I live, as well as lots of other beautiful lights God has hung in the night sky. Let's take a God-moment about . . .

Darker Nights, Brighter Lights

Our word from the Word of God comes from Philippians 2, beginning at verse 15. "Become blameless and pure, children of God without fault in a crooked and depraved generation, in which you shine like stars in the universe as you hold out the word of life." This verse describes a pretty dark background. In fact, some of these words in the original Greek are very revealing. They talk about a world that is actually crooked, like a road that has many turns in it. It is a world that is misshapen, like a pot that did not turn out right on the potter's wheel. In other words, we are living in a twisted generation. We are surrounded by people who have a twisted view of love, sex, marriage, success, and fun. They have a twisted view of God and of the value of human life. We could spend most of our energy just shaking our heads and saying, "It sure is dark. Terrible night out there, isn't it?" Or we can be a high-magnitude star. That night in South Africa, I found out that the darker the night is, the brighter the light shines. Jesus says, "Shine in this, like stars in the universe." If we really act like Jesus, we will stand out in that darkness like never before.

This is not a time to retreat, it is a time for Christians to charge. It is no time for Jesus' disciples to run and hide in a Christian cocoon. This is a time to invade a dark office, a dark school, or a dark neighborhood with the Jesus difference. Because it is darker, it doesn't take much to stand out—a smile, a second question that shows you care, praying with someone who is hurting, letting other people go first, staying cool when everybody else panics. Those simple things will stand out. It is easier to live radically for Christ in a world that is clearly black and white than in one that's gray, but you can't compromise. The Bible says you need to be pure and blameless. Every time a Christian compromises, whether it's the truth, sexual purity, or commitment, the people around lose hope that there really is any light. They think it's all dark until they see a star, a Jesus person.

Hold out the Word of Life. Jesus looks better and stands out more against this dark sky than He ever has before. You are a bright star in an otherwise dark universe. Don't ever let your light go out or your star fall.

Sometimes I joke about my age. For example, some archaeologists just discovered the remains of my high school. Actually, having birthdays never bothers me. Thirty didn't. Forty didn't. Fifty didn't. What did affect me, though, was a memorial service for a friend of mine. I never thought about how old he was until I looked at the program at the service. At the very top, it gave his name, and then it gave his year of birth. Well, that really hit me because it was the year I was born. Let's take a God-moment about . . .

Not Enough Days

No matter what year you were born, someone born that year died this year. When that happens, it makes you remember that you never know how many days you have left, whether you're young or very old. Some people know they have a terminal condition, and the doctor says, "You have three months, six months, or a year to live." Some of us may have that or less, but we just haven't had it announced to us.

Our word from the Word of God comes from Ephesians 5:15–17. "Be very careful, then, how you live—not as unwise but as wise, making the most of every opportunity, because the days are evil. Therefore do not be foolish, but understand what the Lord's will is." There are several ways you can translate this verse that talks about making the most of every opportunity. It all comes out to about the same meaning. One common translation from the Greek is "buying up the time." Going in there like something's on sale and saying, "I have to get this." Or better yet, acting like there's a shortage of it. "I better gather this up and get as much of this as I can while I can."

These verses hit me at the memorial service. I began to think, "There's not a day to waste before I keep my appointment with God." It's amazing how time flies by. I remember talking to a freshman high school football player one day on the field, and I said, "Chris, you're going to blink your eyes and you're going to be a senior, and you're going to wonder where your high

250   THE MISSION YOU WERE MADE FOR

school years went." He said, "Yeah, yeah." Four years later, he said, "I don't know if you remember what you said when I was a freshman, but where did it go? I was just a freshman the other day." Parents wake up and see most of their shaping time with their kids is suddenly gone. Where did it go? You get to mid-life, and some people have a crisis because they look and say, "What have I really accomplished?" Well, there's no point in looking back, but let's look at the future. Whether you have years, months, weeks, or days, it's yet to be captured.

How can you make the greatest difference in the time you have left? We can't waste a conversation, a day, a family time, or an opportunity to speak about Christ. We have to make the

---

No matter what year you were born, someone born that year died this year. When that happens, it makes you remember that you never know how many days you have left. How can you make the greatest difference in the time you have left?

---

most of every opportunity, living wisely, making sure we know what God's will is. This doesn't mean that we become some intense, driven robot, but we're positive God-pleasers who have a strong sense of purpose and of making time count. Now, don't settle for just doing things with the flow of high school, the flow of college, the flow of people in your career, or the flow of circumstances. Take charge of your future. Unload what you need to. Reorganize in order to make a greater difference. Start taking some first steps toward a mission that you feel God may have for you to fulfill in people's lives. If He's impressed a need on your heart or a kind of ministry to be involved with, do a little of it. Start walking down that road. Start making the most of every opportunity, and pray this powerful prayer: "Lord, I want to make more of a difference with my life than I have up to this point." He'll honor that, and He'll answer it in an exciting way. Don't be afraid of any risks God asks you to take in order to obey Him. How true that old poem is. "Only one life, 'twill soon be past; only what's done for Christ will last."